Oracle Certification Prep

Study Guide for

1Z0-460: Oracle Linux 6 Implementation Essentials

Matthew Morris

Study Guide for Oracle Linux 6: Implementation Essentials (Exam 1Z0-460) Rev 1.0

ISBN-13: 978-1492895602
ISBN-10: 1492895601

Table of Contents

What to expect from the test 10

What to Expect from this Study Guide 11

Additional Study Resources 12

Introduction to Oracle Linux 13

Describe the Oracle Linux Product 13

Describe the relationship between Oracle Linux and Red Hat Enterprise Linux (RHEL) 13

Describe Oracle Linux strategy and Oracle's commitment to Linux 14

Describe Oracle's Unbreakable Enterprise Kernel 15

Describe the key differences between Unbreakable Enterprise Kernel and Red Hat Compatible Kernel 15

Installing Oracle Linux 6 18

Describe how to obtain Oracle Linux Operating System software 18

Describe Oracle Linux Install options 19

Describe automating installs with Kickstart 19

Perform an installation of Oracle Linux 6 22

Perform post installation steps and verification 24

Describe all key Oracle Linux related sites like edelivery, ULN, oss, public-yum etc. 25

Linux Boot Process 27

Describe the Linux boot process 27

Configure the GRand Unified Bootloader (GRUB) bootloader 28

Configure kernel boot parameters 29

Boot different kernels (Red Hat Compatible Kernel and Unbreakable Enterprise Kernel) 30

Describe the /sbin/init program, Linux runlevels and runlevel scripts .. 32

Examine the /etc/rc.d directory 33

Oracle Linux System Configuration and Process Management 35

Describe the /etc/sysconfig directory 35

Examine the /proc file system 36

Describe the sysfs file system 37

Use the sysctl utility 40

Display and change the current values of kernel parameters using sysctl 41

Use the ulimit command and the set parameters 42

Find and control running programs with ps, top, kill, and nice 46

Use the jobs, fg and bg commands to view and access several tasks 50

Oracle Linux Package Management 54

Describe Oracle Linux package management 54

Use the RPM utility 55

Describe the Oracle Public YUM Server 57

Describe and configure YUM repositories 58

Use the YUM utility 59

Describe the Unbreakable Linux Network (ULN) 62

Switch from Red Hat Network (RHN) to ULN 64

Install the Oracle RDBMS Server 11gR2 Pre-install RPM package for Oracle Linux 6 66

Set up a local YUM repository 67

Ksplice Zero Downtime Updates 69

Describe the purpose of Ksplice 69

Describe the benefits of Ksplice 69

Describe how Ksplice works 70

Configure and use Ksplice 71

Manage Ksplice systems 72

Automate tasks and System Logging 75

Describe available automated tasks utilities 75

Configure cron jobs and use crontab utility 75

Configure anacron jobs 77

Observe contents of rsyslog configuration file 79

Describe rsyslog actions and templates 81

Configure rsyslog to log debug messages 82

User and Group Administration 85

Create users and groups using command-line utilities 85

Use the id command to verify user information and manually review passwd and group files 88

Configure password aging 90

Use the User Manager GUI tool 93

Describe LDAP and NIS authentication options 96

Perform basic Pluggable Authentication Modules (PAM) configuration and configure LDAP authentication 99

Oracle Linux File Systems and Storage Administration 103

Describe disk partitioning and disk partitioning utilities 103

Describe supported file system types (ext2, ext3, ext4, Vfat, btrfs,ocfs2,nfs) 105

Perform file system creation, mounting and maintenance 108

Manage swap space 112

Use archiving and compression tools like tar, cpio, zip and gzip 114

Describe ASMLib package 117
Describe Clusterware add-on package 118
Network Administration 119
Describe network interface configuration files 119
Use command line network interface utilities 121
Use the NetworkManager tool to configure network connections 125
Use the system-config-network utility 128
Examine files in /etc/sysconfig/network-scripts 129
Set up bonding 131
Set up a VLAN and a bonded VLAN 133
Configure Iptables and routing 134
Basic Security Administration 137
Describe SELinux modes, policies, booleans, and contexts 137
Enable and disable SELinux configuration 139
Manage access to system services using Service configuration tool ... 141
Use the Firewall configuration tool 143
Configure iptables rules 145
Verify Common Vulnerabilities and Exposures (CVE) security updates are up to date 149
Oracle Linux System Monitoring and Troubleshooting 151
Use OSWatcher tool and configure to start at boot time 151
Use sosreport 153
Use sar, strace, iostat, tcpdump and ethereal tools 155
Use vmstat and top 164
Describe DTrace tool 167
Set up kdump / netconsole 168
Verify proper creation of vmcore by kdump using crash 170

Describe OS management capabilities of both Opscenter and EM management for Oracle Linux 172

What to expect from the test

The test consists of 71 multiple choice or multiple answer questions and you will have 120 minutes to complete it. The passing score listed on Oracle Education at this time is 62%, but as with all Oracle certification tests, they note it is subject to change.

The topics on this exam are a mixed bag. About 60% are about fairly generic Linux skills and knowledge that would fit right in with the CompTIA Linux+ exam. Another 10% are Linux topics that have close ties to Red Hat Enterprise Linux, Fedora, or Oracle Linux. Another 10% is completely specific to Oracle Linux. The final 10% of the topics are essentially Oracle marketing (like 'describe the benefits of Ksplice').

If you are knowledgeable about Linux, and in particular knowledgeable of Red Hat Enterprise Linux (or Fedora), then you have an excellent starting point for on this exam. The topics of the exam are more focused than typical Linux exams such as those from CompTIA or the LPI. Partly that is because the Oracle Linux exams assume that the system will be used to house an Oracle server. The exam doesn't cover common utilities like sendmail or cups because those are not functions that would generally be critical for a Linux server intended to host an Oracle database. This exam is even more focused because it is intended for Oracle implementers. These individuals may install and configure an Oracle Linux server, but will not be the system administrator in charge of maintaining it.

I expected this test to be fairly simple because it is an 'Essentials' exam and I have a fair amount of Linux experience. However, the exam got much deeper into specifics than I expected. You must memorize common parameters for the various utilities (there is no way to call up 'man' to refresh your memory). Likewise you must not only recognize common configuration files, but also be able to determine their locations, contents, and what utilities update them. Much of the information required for the exam I usually get from the Linux console when required. However, to have the best chance of passing this exam, the information must be committed to memory.

What to Expect from this Study Guide

This document is built around the subject matter topics that Oracle Education has indicated will be tested. This book contains material from several Oracle and Red Hat documentation sources along with information from Oracle websites and results from commands executed against and files pulled from an Oracle Linux 6 server. The guide covers a significant percentage of the information and operations that you must be familiar with in order to pass the exam.

What this guide is intended to do is present the information that will be covered on the exam at the level it will likely be asked. The guide assumes that you have at least some experience with the Linux operating system. No book in and of itself is a substitute for hands-on experience. You need to spend some time working with a Linux installation before scheduling this exam. Oracle Linux is free to download and install. Oracle VM Virtualbox is free to download and install. That means that with just about any PC or laptop, you can install Virtualbox and then install Oracle Linux onto a virtual machine. You don't need to buy anything or have a spare machine that can be blown away to make a practice Linux box. Discounting the download time for the two (I have no idea how fast your Internet connection is), you can have a virtual Linux server running in less than a half hour. Having a server available to practice with the commands and utilities as you read through this guide will add considerable value to your study time.

The goal of this guide is to present to you the concepts and information most likely to be the subject of test questions, and to do so in a very compact format that will allow you to read through it more than once to reinforce the information. If you find much of the information is completely new -- you need to supplement this guide with other sources of study materials. The information in this guide will not help you nearly as much if you do not have enough knowledge to put it into context. If you have a fair amount of experience with Linux, this guide should provide you with enough information specific to the exam to give you a reasonable chance of passing.

Additional Study Resources

The companion website to this series is www.oraclecertificationprep.com. The site contains many additional resources that can be used to study for this exam (and others). From the entry page of the website, click on the 'Exams' button, and then select the link for this test. The Exam Details page contains links to the following information sources:

- Applicable Oracle documentation.
- Third-party books relevant to the exam.
- White papers and articles on Oracle Learning Library on topics covered in the exam.
- Articles on the Web that may be useful for the exam.
- Videos at YouTube and other sites that provide relevant tutorials.

The website will never link to unauthorized content such as brain dumps or illegal content such as copyrighted material made available without the consent of the author. I cannot guarantee the accuracy of the content links. While I have located the data and scanned it to ensure that it is relevant to the given exam, I did not write it and have not proofread it from a technical standpoint. The material on the Oracle Learning Library is almost certain to be completely accurate and most of the other links come from highly popular Oracle support websites and are created by experienced Oracle professionals.

I recommend that you use more than one source of study materials whenever you are preparing for a certification. Reading information presented from multiple different viewpoints can help to give you a more complete picture of any given topic. The links on the website can help you to do this. Fully understanding the information covered in this certification is not just valuable for getting a passing score – it will also help your career. In the long run, any knowledge you gain from this certification will provide more benefits than a piece of paper or line on your resume.

Introduction to Oracle Linux

Describe the Oracle Linux Product

The Oracle Linux distribution is a high-performance operating system that is compatible with the Red Hat Enterprise Linux distribution. It is free to download and distribute, including all source code, binaries, patches and updates. The code has been optimized for use as a database server and for use in Oracle systems such as Oracle Exadata Database Machine, Oracle Exalytics In-Memory Machine, Oracle Exalogic Elastic Cloud, and Oracle Database Appliance.

Oracle Linux tracks the mainline Red Hat Enterprise Distribution closely, ensuring that updates and enhancements are rapidly available to customers. The kernel is designed to deliver superior performance, data integrity, security, and application uptime. It is the only Linux OS that offers Zero Downtime Patching. The Linux kernel can be updated while running without requiring a reboot.

Oracle Linux offer the choice of two kernels. The Red Hat Compatible Kernel (RHCK) offers 100% compatibility with the kernel supplied with Red Hat Enterprise Linux and identical capabilities. The default kernel used with Oracle Linux 6 (and versions from 5.6 onwards) is the Unbreakable Enterprise Kernel (UEK). The UEK provides several advanced functions not available with the RHCK.

Describe the relationship between Oracle Linux and Red Hat Enterprise Linux (RHEL)

Oracle Linux is a tracking distribution of Red Hat Enterprise Linux (RHEL). RHEL is in turn, derived from the Fedora Core project. The Oracle Linux distribution first began in October 2006 and it has full user-space compatibility with RHEL. Since the original distribution, no incompatibilities have been found between Oracle Linux and Red Hat.

The public git repositories with the full history of the Oracle kernel development can be accessed at the following URLs:

- http://oss.oracle.com/git
- https://oss.oracle.com/git/?p=redpatch.git

Any time a new version of Red Hat Enterprise is released, an Oracle Linux distribution will follow shortly with the same enhancements. From the table below, you can see that the Oracle releases are usually within a couple of weeks of the Red Hat release:

RHEL 6 GA	11/9/2010	Oracle Linux 6.0	2/12/2011
RHEL 6 Update 1	5/19/2011	Oracle Linux 6.1	6/1/2011
RHEL 6 Update 2	12/6/2011	Oracle Linux 6.2	12/20/2011
RHEL 6 Update 3	6/20/2012	Oracle Linux 6.3	6/29/2012
RHEL 6 Update 4	2/21/2013	Oracle Linux 6.4	2/28/2013

Describe Oracle Linux strategy and Oracle's commitment to Linux

Oracle has committed to using the Oracle Linux distribution as their operating system of choice. They offer a complete Linux-based solution stack—applications, middleware, database, management tools, operating system and hardware. Oracle invests in continuous and comprehensive testing of Oracle Linux on multiple hardware platforms. Critical bug fixes are released faster to provide maximum stability and minimize vulnerability.

Oracle provides industry-leading global support for the Linux operating system. They provide enterprise-class support for both Oracle Linux and Red Hat Enterprise Linux. RHEL support is available whether or not a customer owns any Oracle products. Coverage is provided by the world's largest global software support team 24-by-7 in 145 countries and 20 local languages.

Describe Oracle's Unbreakable Enterprise Kernel

The Unbreakable Enterprise Kernel (UEK) is designed to provide improvements beyond the capabilities provided by the standard Red hat Enterprise Kernel. The current version of Oracle's UEK is the second major release. UEK Release 2 is based on the mainline Linux kernel version 3.0.36. The kernel identifies itself as version 2.6.39 to avoid potential issues with some low-level system tools that depend on the kernel version number. The reported version does not affect regular applications.

The UEK contains optimizations developed in collaboration with Oracle's Database, Middleware, and Hardware engineering teams. The changes are designed to ensure stability and optimal performance for enterprise systems. Oracle Linux is the base operating system for the Oracle Exadata and Exalogic systems. The Unbreakable Enterprise Kernel contains enhancements and improvements to improve performance on these large systems, resulting in better scalability, improved memory management and better Infiniband support.

All UEK contributions and patches on top of the mainline kernel are open source and available in the following git tree:

https://oss.oracle.com/git/?p=linux-uek-2.6.39.git;a=summary

Oracle Linux with the Unbreakable Enterprise Kernel is used exclusively for all of Oracle's build and QA systems. It is also the only OS used in Linux benchmarks that Oracle participates in.

Describe the key differences between Unbreakable Enterprise Kernel and Red Hat Compatible Kernel

Some of the key differences in the Unbreakable Enterprise Kernel include:

- **BTRFS File System** -- BTRFS allows for flexible storage management without requiring a separate volume manager. RAID support is built in to the file system and ensures data integrity by using redundancy and checksums. It also supports lightweight copies/clones of files or directories with snapshots as well as online data compression.

- **Performance and Scalability** -- The UEK has been tweaked to perform better and faster on systems with multiple CPUs and large amounts of main memory. Improvements have been made to the scheduler, memory management, file system layers and the networking stack.
- **Memory Compaction** -- External memory fragmentation is reduced by attempting to move used pages into a new large block of contiguous pages. This makes it easier for the Linux kernel to allocate bigger chunks of memory and reduces the amount of I/O required to satisfy large page allocations.
- **Transmit Packet Steering** -- Outgoing network traffic is spread across CPUs on multi-queue devices to improve network throughput.
- **Cgroups Improvements** -- UEK Release 2 added new controllers that provide the ability to control disk bandwidth allocation and to set upper read/write limits to a group of processes. It also includes a new feature that supports "process grouping", allowing changes to the way a process scheduler assigns shares of CPU time to each process. This can improve the responsiveness of applications under certain load conditions.
- **OCFS2 Improvements** -- The Oracle Cluster File System has had several refinements in UEK Release 2 to improve performance and reduce overhead.

The Unbreakable Enterprise Kernel includes several features which are still under development, but are made available for testing/evaluation purposes. These include the following:

- **Linux Containers** -- Safely and securely run multiple applications or instances of an operating system on a single host without the risk of interference between each instance.
- **Dtrace** -- This is a comprehensive dynamic tracing framework that was initially developed for the Oracle Solaris operating system. It allows administrators, developers, and service personnel to answer questions about the behavior of the operating system and user programs in real time.

- **Transcendent memory** -- This provides a means to improve physical memory utilization in a virtualized environment by claiming underutilized memory in a system and making it available where it is most needed.

In a nutshell, the primary advantages of the UEK are:

- Can parallelize network and disk IO
- Efficiently runs on systems with many cores and threads and NUMA nodes
- Optimized for solid state
- Transparent Huge Pages (2Mb instead of 4Kb)
- Built-in data integrity
- Improved hardware fault management
- Resource Isolation via Control Groups (Cgroups)
- OCFS2 improvements – Global heartbeat, TRIM support for SSDs
- Xen domU scalability improvements
- Updated Device Drivers
- Improved power management - ACPI 4.0

Installing Oracle Linux 6

Describe how to obtain Oracle Linux Operating System software

You may download, use and distribute Oracle Linux Release 6 free of charge. Installation images are available for download from the Oracle Software Delivery Cloud (http://edelivery.oracle.com/linux). Once Oracle Linux is installed on your system, it is possible to obtain Linux packages from either the Oracle Public Yum server or from the Unbreakable Linux Network (ULN).

There are a images available for several different platforms. The following examples are for x86_64 (64 Bit) hardware:

- **(V37084-01) Oracle Linux Release 6 Update 4 for x86_64 (64 Bit)** -- This is a complete and bootable ISO DVD image. Once burned to DVD, it is possible to use this to boot your server and install Oracle Linux. It can be made available as a virtual DVD-ROM drive under Oracle VM VirtualBox or Oracle VM to boot and install a guest system. Alternately you can make the contents available over a network via NFS or HTTP.
- **(V37088-01) Oracle Linux Release 6 Update 4 Boot ISO image for x86_64 (64 bit)** -- This is an ISO image for the Red Hat Compatible Kernel. This image can be burned to either a DVD or CD and used to boot a server and begin an installation. In order to complete the installation, it is necessary to specify how to access the installation packages.
- **(V37090-01) Oracle Linux Release 6 Update 4 UEK Boot ISO image for x86_64 (64 bit)** -- This is an ISO image for the Unbreakable Enterprise Kernel Release 2. This image can be burned to either a DVD or CD and used to boot a server and begin an installation. In order to complete the installation, it is necessary to specify how to access the installation packages.
- **(V37086-01/V37087-01)** Oracle Linux Release 6 Update 4 source DVD 1/2 -- These are DVD ISO images that contain the source code for the software packages in the release.

Describe Oracle Linux Install options

There are several different possible sources for the RPM packages when installing Oracle Linux onto a new system. Each has advantages and disadvantages. The best solution depends on your situation: the hardware you are installing Linux on, the number of systems being installed, and so forth. The various options include:

- **Boot ISO Image** -- When installing on a Virtualbox -- using the downloaded ISO image as a virtual drive is simple and requires no additional setup.
- **Physical CD or DVD** -- If the system has a CD or DVD drive, you can use that for installation. A recordable DVD has enough storage capacity for a full, bootable installation ISO image. A recordable CD has the capacity for a boot ISO image (about 200 MB), but not for a full, bootable installation ISO image.
- **Network Installation Server** -- It is possible to set up a network installation server to host the RPM packages. The server requires approximately 3.5 GB of storage space free to hold the full Oracle Linux Release 6 installation DVD image. The server must be configured to use either HTTP or NFS to serve the image files to the target systems on which you want to install Oracle Linux 6.
- **Bootable USB Memory Stick** -- If the system's firmware supports booting from a USB drive, you can create a boot image on a USB memory stick. The USB stick can then be used to boot the system and start the installation. A USB boot image does not contain any installation packages so you will be prompted to specify the location of the full installation image during the install.

Describe automating installs with Kickstart

During every Oracle Linux installation, the choices made during the process are recorded in a Kickstart configuration file, /root/anaconda-ks.cfg. This file can be used to repeat the installation on another systsem exactly, or it can be customized to perform different actions. The Kickstart Configurator tool, system-config-kickstart, can be used either to create a new file or modify an existing one.

There are several sections to a Kickstart file, some of which are optional. The top part of the file is for the basic installation options such as the language, keyboard type, etc. It also defines the system storage configuration. An example of this section follows (lines starting with # are comments):

```
# Kickstart file automatically generated by anaconda.

#version=DEVEL
install
cdrom
lang en_US.UTF-8
keyboard us
network --onboot no --device eth0 --bootproto dhcp --noipv6
rootpw  --iscrypted $6$R1Gny1CDrY1X3LXt$2zX6HuoKCTnCd7Kzbwk
R2d.j.LCLzjXemd5U7zBrhnt51AE6P5zmv2plc7sg8xCZGKGEN8cHnTZdiX
firewall --service=ssh
authconfig --enableshadow --passalgo=sha512
selinux --enforcing
timezone --utc America/New_York
bootloader --location=mbr --driveorder=sda --append="
crashkernel=auto rhgb quiet"
# The following is the partition information you requested
# Note that any partitions you deleted are not expressed
# here so unless you clear all partitions first, this is
# not guaranteed to work
#clearpart --linux --drives=sda

#part /boot --fstype=ext4 --size=500
#part pv.008002 --grow --size=1

#volgroup vg_matthew --pesize=4096 pv.008002
#logvol / --fstype=ext4 --name=lv_root --vgname=vg_matthew
--grow --size=1024 --maxsize=51200
#logvol swap --name=lv_swap --vgname=vg_matthew --grow
--size=2016 --maxsize=2016
```

The file will also contain a Packages section (starting with the '%packages' keyword) which lists the software packages that will be added to the system during install. Package group names are prefixed with the @ character and individual packages without no prefix. If a package name is prefixed by the - character, then it will not be installed.

Following is a partial listing of a packages section:

```
%packages
@base
@client-mgmt-tools
@core
@debugging
@basic-desktop
...
certmonger
pam_krb5
krb5-workstation
libXmu
perl-DBD-SQLite
```

The %packages keyword takes the following options:

- **--ignoredeps** -- Installs the packages without attempting to fix any unresolved dependencies.
- **--ignoremissing** -- Installs the available packages without prompting about missing packages. By default, Kickstart interrupts the installation and asks you whether you want to continue the installation.
- **--resolvedeps** -- Install the packages and prompt if there are any unresolved dependencies.

A Kickstart configuration file can optionally have a pre-installation configuration section. This section, started with the %pre keyword, defines actions to be performed before the installation starts. Examples of pre-installation options are running remote scripts or downloading a list of packages to be installed.

The file can also have a post-installation configuration section (started with the %post keyword) for actions to be taken after the install completes. Post installation tasks are executed in a chroot environment based on the root file system of the newly installed system. You must specify the --nochroot option to %post if you need to access any files that are outside the chroot environment.

When performing an installation using Kickstart, access to the Oracle Linux installation media is required, either on a local CD-ROM drive or hard drive, or over the network using HTTP or NFS. The steps to install using Kickstart are:

1. Boot the system from a bootable medium.
2. If you have not customized the boot medium to use Kickstart, use the ks option to specify the location of the Kickstart file.
3. If the Kickstart configuration does not specify the installation method, insert the installation DVD or make the installation image available to the system when prompted.

Perform an installation of Oracle Linux 6

While this section will describe the utilities and steps involved in an installation of Oracle Linux, it is really not the best way to learn about one. If you have never installed Oracle Linux, then you should perform one or more installations on your own. The easiest way to do so is to download Oracle's Virtualbox software and an ISO file of Oracle 6. Then install Virtualbox, create a virtual machine, and install Linux there. What is really nice about using Virtualbox is that you don't need a second machine and you can easily become familiar with the various options of an Oracle Linux install by running an install, then dropping that virtual machine, creating a new one, and trying the install again using different choices.

Oracle Linux uses the same Anaconda installer used by Fedora and Red Hat Enterprise Linux. If you have installed Linux on Fedora or Red Hat, the process is essentially identical for Oracle Linux. Anaconda has the following features:

- Runs in Text or Graphical Mode
- Install from CD, DVD, USB or images on hard disk drive
- Supports HTTP, FTP, NFS installation

On starting an install, you are presented with a screen where you can choose from several options:

- Install or upgrade an existing system
- Install system with basic video driver
- Rescue installed system
- Boot from local drive
- Memory test

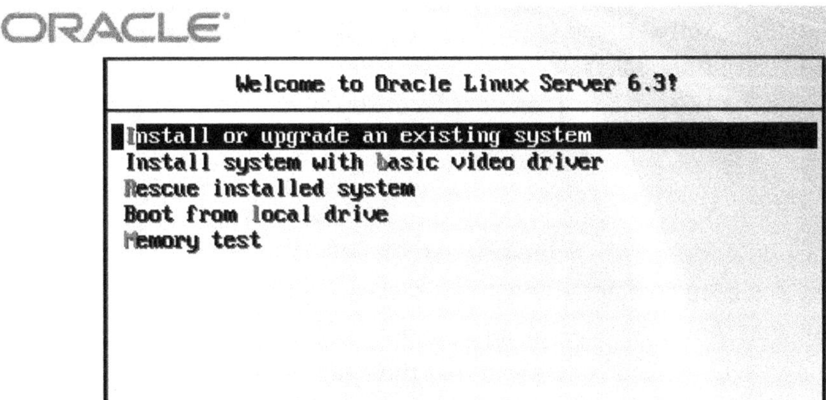

Selecting either of the 'Install' options will ask if you wish to perform a media test. Once the test has been completed (or skipped) the system will load the Linux OS into memory from the installation media and begin the Anaconda install. During the install you will be asked to supply information about your hardware and the options desired for the installation, including:

- Installation language.
- Installation keyboard layout.
- The network interface to use for installation (if any).
- Type of medium to use for installation: DVD, hard disk, NFS, or URL.
- Storage devices on which you intend to install the operating system, such as a local hard disk.

- The fully qualified domain name of the system, or if you intend to use DHCP to provide network settings, just the host name.
- Any other network interface to be configured during installation
- The country and city to use when specifying the time zone.
- The layout of the storage devices on which the Linux file systems will be installed.
- The amount of space required for each file system (/, /boot, /home, /var/tmp, and so on), the file system type, and whether the block device underlying each file system should be encrypted.
- The root user password
- The software packages that should be installed on the system.
- Any optional packages to be installed.
- The URLs of any additional repositories and proxy settings to be used for package installation.

Perform post installation steps and verification

Once you have completed the initial installation, there are several more steps that should be taken. These are optional, but they ensure that all of the packages are up-to-date and that the system is secure. The post-install steps include:

- **Registering with the Unbreakable Linux Network** -- Unbreakable Linux Network (ULN) requires a subscription with Oracle for Linux Support. Registering with ULN is optional, but the network provides Oracle Linux updates and channels for Oracle-specific software packages such as Oracle's ASMlib userspace package and the Oracle Instant Client.
- **Obtaining Errata and Updates from Public Yum** -- Oracle's public yum server requires no subscription and can be used to obtain all errata and updates for Oracle Linux. The public yum server, like ULN, contains updates to the base distribution, but does not include Oracle-specific software. By default, all new installations of Oracle Linux 6 are automatically configured to use the public yum update service. If the system is later registered with ULN, the public yum service is automatically disabled.
- **Obtaining Packages from the Oracle Linux Installation Media** -- The Oracle Linux 6 installation ISO contains distinct repository sources for the Red Hat Compatible Kernel and the Unbreakable

Enterprise Kernel. Once you have completed the install, you can configure yum to use one (or both) repositories from an ISO image of the installation media.

- **Applying Updates** -- After configuring your system to use ULN (or leaving it with the Public Yum default), and any media repositories that yum should use, you should update the installed packages with the 'yum update' command.
- **Configuring the System Firewall** -- If your system is accessible from the Web, you should secure it using a firewall after install. Simple firewall rules can be configured using the Firewall Configuration GUI (systemconfig-firewall) or the text-based version (system-config-firewall-tui). You can use the iptables and ip6tables utilities to configure more complex rules for IPv4 and IPv6.
- **Changing the SELinux Mode** -- SELinux provides additional security to your Oracle Linux server. You can use the Status view of the SELinux Administration GUI (system-config-selinux) to set the default and current SELinux mode. Alternately you can use the commands 'getenforce' and 'setenforce' to see and set the SELinux mode.

Describe all key Oracle Linux related sites like edelivery, ULN, oss, public-yum etc.

- **edelivery** -- The edelivery site is the interface for obtaining Oracle Linux installation media (and Oracle VM as well). It also contains VM templates for both Oracle Linux and Solaris. https://edelivery.oracle.com/linux

- **ULN** -- The Unbreakable Linux Network is Oracle's support site for customers who have an Oracle Linux support contract. It contains Oracle Linux software patches, updates and fixes. It also provides access to the Ksplice zero-downtime updates for Oracle Linux, and provides Errata and CVE Information. Some (but not all) of the services offered by ULN are also available on the Oracle public yum server. https://linux.oracle.com/pls/apex/f?p=101:3

- **Public-Yum** -- The Oracle public yum server is free to use and allows you to install the latest Oracle Linux packages via a yum client. The pubic yum server is offered freely by Oracle but without support of any kind.
  http://public-yum.oracle.com/

- **OSS** -- The OSS portal contains information about all of the Free and/or Open Source Software from Oracle. This includes Oracle's Linux projects but is not restricted to it. The site contains information about Oracle's work on other open source projects such as MySQL, Virtualbox and the GlassFish Server Open Source Edition.
  https://oss.oracle.com/

- **Oracle Linux Product Page** -- The Oracle Linux product page contains largely marketing-related information about Oracle Linux. However, is contains some useful information and links to more details and white papers.
  http://oracle.com/linux

- **Oracle Linux 6 Documentation** -- Contains links to all of the Oracle Linux 6 documentation in HTML, PDF, and ePub formats.
  http://docs.oracle.com/cd/E37670_01/

- **Ksplice Signup** -- Allows you to sign up for a 30-day trial of Ksplice.
  https://www.ksplice.com/ol-signup

Linux Boot Process

Describe the Linux boot process

The Linux boot process is the sequence of steps involved from initial power being applied to the system until the operating system is ready for use. In Linux, there are six basic steps involved in the boot process.

- **BIOS** – The system BIOS performs hardware checks and launches the first stage boot loader on the Master Boot Record of the primary hard disk
- **MBR** -- The Master Boot Record launches the second stage boot loader from the /boot/ partition
- **GRUB** -- The GRand Unified Boot loader loads and executes the Kernel and initrd images using the /boot/grub/grub.conf file
- **Kernel** -- The kernel initializes and configures the hardware, mounts the root file system and executes the /sbin/init program.
- **Init** -- The init program runs the /etc/rc.d/rc.sysinit script, which executes all steps required for system initialization
- **Init Runlevel** -- Depending on init level setting, the system will execute the programs from one of the /etc/rc.d directories

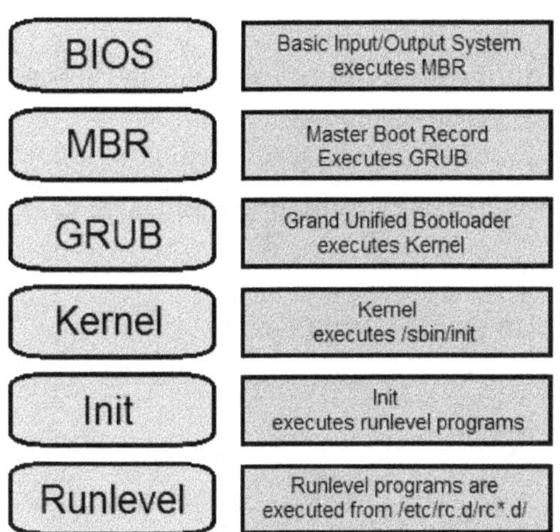

Configure the GRand Unified Bootloader (GRUB) bootloader

A boot loader is the first software program that runs when a computer starts. Its function is to load and transfer control to an operating system kernel. The kernel will then initialize the rest of the operating system. The default Oracle Linux boot loader for the x86 platform is GRUB. The actions of GRUB are controlled by the contents of its configuration file: '/boot/grub/grub.conf. The grub.conf file can contain a large number of commands. Definitions for five of the most common are:

- **Title** -- A GRUB file can contain multiple entries for 'title', each of which represents an available kernel that the bootloader can select on startup.
- **Default** -- The bootable kernels are numbered from top to bottom starting with zero. A default value of zero means that GRUB will boot, by default, the first kernel entry.
- **Timeout** -- This directive determines how long GRUB will wait for keyboard input before booting the default kernel. Pressing any key within the timeout period will display the GRUB menu. A timeout value of five indicates that GRUB will wait five seconds. A timeout of zero makes the default kernel boot with no waiting period.
- **Splashimage** -- Oracle Linux hides the boot process with a boot splash screen. The 'splashimage=' directive specifies the splash screen to use. Pressing Esc during the boot process will cause the output from the boot process to be displayed.
- **Hiddenmenu** -- The 'hiddenmenu' directive tells GRUB not to display the GRUB menu. This directive has no argument.

The following is an example of a GRUB configuration file. It contains two bootable kernels, one for the Unbreakable Enterprise Kernel and the second for the Red Hat Compatible Kernel.

```
# grub.conf generated by anaconda
#
#boot=/dev/sda
default=0
timeout=5
splashimage=(hd0,0)/grub/splash.xpm.gz
hiddenmenu
title Oracle Linux Server-uek (2.6.39-200.24.1.el6uek.x86_64)
        root (hd0,0)
        kernel /vmlinuz-2.6.39-200.24.1.el6uek.x86_64 ro
          root=/dev/mapper/vg_matthew-lv_root rd_NO_LUKS
          LANG=en_US.UTF-8 rd_LVM_LV=vg_matthew/lv_swap
          rd_NO_MD SYSFONT=latarcyrheb-sun16
          rd_LVM_LV=vg_matthew/lv_root  KEYBOARDTYPE=pc
          KEYTABLE=us rd_NO_DM rhgb quiet
        initrd /initramfs-2.6.39-200.24.1.el6uek.x86_64.img
title Oracle Linux Server (2.6.32-279.el6.x86_64)
        root (hd0,0)
        kernel /vmlinuz-2.6.32-279.el6.x86_64 ro
          root=/dev/mapper/vg_matthew-lv_root rd_NO_LUKS
          LANG=en_US.UTF-8 rd_LVM_LV=vg_matthew/lv_swap
          rd_NO_MD SYSFONT=latarcyrheb-sun16
          crashkernel=auto rd_LVM_LV=vg_matthew/lv_root
          KEYBOARDTYPE=pc KEYTABLE=us rd_NO_DM rhgb quiet
        initrd /initramfs-2.6.32-279.el6.x86_64.img
```

Configure kernel boot parameters

Most of the commands in the grub.conf file have just a single value. The kernel command is the exception and has an entire string of them. The first value after the kernel keyword is the kernel file that will be loaded. The other values set boot time parameters for the kernel being loaded. Some of the options are obvious, such as the ones setting the language, system font, keyboard type, and keyboard language, while others are more cryptic. Definitions for several of these parameters are:

- **root=** -- Defines the root filesystem.
- **ro** -- Mount root device read-only on boot.
- **rw** -- Mount root device read-write on boot (the default).
- **initrd=** -- Specifies the location of the initial ramdisk.
- **init=** -- Run specified binary instead of /sbin/init
- **quiet** -- Suppresses display of kernel messages during decompression
- **rhgb** -- Red Hat Graphical Boot display

```
title Oracle Linux Server-uek (2.6.39-200.24.1.el6uek.x86_64)
        root (hd0,0)
        kernel /vmlinuz-2.6.39-200.24.1.el6uek.x86_64 ro
          root=/dev/mapper/vg_matthew-lv_root rd_NO_LUKS
          LANG=en_US.UTF-8 rd_LVM_LV=vg_matthew/lv_swap
          rd_NO_MD SYSFONT=latarcyrheb-sun16
          rd_LVM_LV=vg_matthew/lv_root  KEYBOARDTYPE=pc
          KEYTABLE=us rd_NO_DM rhgb quiet
        initrd /initramfs-2.6.39-200.24.1.el6uek.x86_64.img
```

Boot different kernels (Red Hat Compatible Kernel and Unbreakable Enterprise Kernel)

Oracle Linux 6 ships with both Oracle's Unbreakable Enterprise Kernel (UEK) and Red Hat Compatible Kernel (RHCK). By default, the Oracle Linux 6.3 release boots with the Unbreakable Enterprise Kernel Release 2. This is the kernel Oracle recommends using for all enterprise applications. However, you can choose to use the Red Hat Compatible Kernel instead if desired. The uname command can be used to determine the current kernel being used by your server. In this case, the server is running 2.6.39-200.24.1.el6uek.x86_64. The 'uek' indicates that it is currently the Unbreakable Enterprise Kernel.

```
[root@matthew ~]# uname -a
Linux matthew.example.com 2.6.39-200.24.1.el6uek.x86_64 #1 SMP
Sat Jun 23 02:39:07 EDT 2012 x86_64 x86_64 x86_64 GNU/Linux
```

From the grub.conf file examined earlier, the two title sections represented the UEK and RHCK kernels:

```
title Oracle Linux Server-uek (2.6.39-200.24.1.el6uek.x86_64)
        root (hd0,0)
        kernel /vmlinuz-2.6.39-200.24.1.el6uek.x86_64 ro
          root=/dev/mapper/vg_matthew-lv_root rd_NO_LUKS
          LANG=en_US.UTF-8 rd_LVM_LV=vg_matthew/lv_swap
          rd_NO_MD SYSFONT=latarcyrheb-sun16
          rd_LVM_LV=vg_matthew/lv_root  KEYBOARDTYPE=pc
          KEYTABLE=us rd_NO_DM rhgb quiet
        initrd /initramfs-2.6.39-200.24.1.el6uek.x86_64.img
```

```
title Oracle Linux Server (2.6.32-279.el6.x86_64)
        root (hd0,0)
        kernel /vmlinuz-2.6.32-279.el6.x86_64 ro
          root=/dev/mapper/vg_matthew-lv_root rd_NO_LUKS
          LANG=en_US.UTF-8 rd_LVM_LV=vg_matthew/lv_swap
          rd_NO_MD SYSFONT=latarcyrheb-sun16
          crashkernel=auto rd_LVM_LV=vg_matthew/lv_root
          KEYBOARDTYPE=pc KEYTABLE=us rd_NO_DM rhgb quiet
        initrd /initramfs-2.6.32-279.el6.x86_64.img
```

The file as configured has the default command set to 0, so the first (UEK) kernel boots by default. Changing the default to 1 will make the second kernel vmlinuz-2.6.32-279.el6.x86_64 the default. Because there is no uek in the kernel version, we know this is the Red Hat Compatible Kernel. Alternately, you could leave the default to 0, but select the RHCK kernel during the boot process during the GRUB timeout period. After rebooting with the new kernel, uname shows that we are running the Red Hat Compatible Kernel.

```
[root@matthew ~]# uname -a
Linux matthew.example.com 2.6.32-279.el6.x86_64 #1 SMP
Thu Jun 21 15:00:18 EDT 2012 x86_64 x86_64 x86_64 GNU/Linux
```

If you change your default boot kernel from the UEK, there is a second file that you must consider when you installing a new version of the kernel package. The /etc/sysconfig/kernel file specifies defaults when updating the kernel. The default kernel file from an Oracle Linux 6.3 system is shown below. As shown, it determines that the UEK kernel package will be the default kernel and when you install a new updated version of UEK kernel that new version will be selected as default kernel to boot the system.

```
# UPDATEDEFAULT specifies if new-kernel-pkg should make
# new kernels the default
UPDATEDEFAULT=yes

# DEFAULTKERNEL specifies the default kernel package type
DEFAULTKERNEL=kernel-uek
```

If you must use the Red Hat Compatible Kernel as your default, then the grub.conf file should be changed and you should also modify the /etc/sysconfig/kernel file. You should change the DEFAULTKERNEL from 'kernel-uek' to 'kernel' so that any time a new version of the kernel is installed, the RHCK version will be set as the default.

Describe the /sbin/init program, Linux runlevels and runlevel scripts

The '/sbin/init' program (sometimes called simply init) is the fifth step in the Linux boot process. It is called by the kernel using a hard-coded filename. If the kernel is unable to start the init process, a kernel panic will result. Init coordinates the remainder of the boot process and configures the environment for the user. Init is the first actual process started during booting of the computer system. It is a daemon process that runs continuously until the system is shut down. It is the direct or indirect ancestor of all other processes. In addition, any processes orphaned while the system is running will be adopted by the init process. Init is typically assigned process identifier 1.

The first task of init is to run the /etc/rc.d/rc.sysinit script. This script sets up the network, mounts the /proc file system, checks the file systems, and executes other steps required for system initialization. Next, the init process runs the /etc/inittab script. The inittab script defines how the system should be set up for each init runlevel.

The runlevels in SysV describe certain states of a machine, characterized by the processes that are run. The runlevels in Oracle Linux 6 are:

- **0** -- Halt
- **1** -- Single User Mode
- **2** -- Multiuser, without NFS
- **3** -- Full Multi-user text mode
- **4** -- Not used
- **5** -- Full Multi-user Graphical Mode
- **6** -- Reboot

Runlevels are defined by the services listed in the System V /etc/rc.d/rc(x).d/ directory, where (x) is the number of the runlevel. The runlevel system provides a standard process for controlling which programs should be launched or halted by init when initializing a runlevel. The /etc/rc.d/ directory contains all of the configuration files for the System V init. The default runlevel for the system is defined in the /etc/inittab file:

```
# inittab is only used by upstart for the default runlevel.
#
# ADDING OTHER CONFIGURATION HERE WILL HAVE NO EFFECT ON YOUR SYSTEM.
#
# System initialization is started by /etc/init/rcS.conf
#
# Individual runlevels are started by /etc/init/rc.conf
#
# Ctrl-Alt-Delete is handled by /etc/init/control-alt-delete.conf
#
# Terminal gettys are handled by /etc/init/tty.conf and /etc/init/serial.conf,
# with configuration in /etc/sysconfig/init.
#
# For information on how to write upstart event handlers, or how
# upstart works, see init(5), init(8), and initctl(8).
#
# Default runlevel. The runlevels used are:
#   0 - halt (Do NOT set initdefault to this)
#   1 - Single user mode
#   2 - Multiuser, without NFS (The same as 3, if you do not have networking)
#   3 - Full multiuser mode
#   4 - unused
#   5 - X11
#   6 - reboot (Do NOT set initdefault to this)
#
id:5:initdefault:
```

Examine the /etc/rc.d directory

The directory /etc/rc.d contains a set of directories named rc0.d, rc1.d, rc2.d, rc3.d, rc4.d, rc5.d, and rc6.d. The system uses these directories to control the services to be started. It also contains the files rc.local and rc.sysinit.

```
[root@matthew rc.d]# ls -l
total 60
drwxr-xr-x. 2 root root  4096 Sep 11 16:45 init.d
-rwxr-xr-x. 1 root root  2617 Jun 22  2012 rc
drwxr-xr-x. 2 root root  4096 Sep 11 16:45 rc0.d
drwxr-xr-x. 2 root root  4096 Sep 11 16:45 rc1.d
drwxr-xr-x. 2 root root  4096 Sep 11 16:45 rc2.d
drwxr-xr-x. 2 root root  4096 Sep 11 16:45 rc3.d
```

```
drwxr-xr-x. 2 root root  4096 Sep 11 16:45 rc4.d
drwxr-xr-x. 2 root root  4096 Sep 11 16:45 rc5.d
drwxr-xr-x. 2 root root  4096 Sep 11 16:45 rc6.d
-rwxr-xr-x. 1 root root   220 Jun 22  2012 rc.local
-rwxr-xr-x. 1 root root 19574 Jun 22  2012 rc.sysinit
```

The init program executes the /etc/rc.d/rc.sysinit script. The rc.sysinit script is too long to show in this guide, but you should take a look at the file in an Oracle Linux 6 system. It sets up the network, mounts /proc, checks the file systems, and executes all other steps required for system initialization. Once rc.sysinit has completed, init then looks at the /etc/inittab file to determine the default runlevel. Based on the value, it will run the scripts in the appropriate directory under /etc/rc.d. The default runlevel in the file from the previous section is 5, so the scripts in the /etc/rc.d/rc.5 will be executed to set up Oracle Linux for that runlevel. After all of the runlevel scripts have been executed, init will execute the /etc/rc.d/rc.local script. In this script you can place custom initialization actions of your own.

```
[root@matthew rc5.d]# ls
K01smartd         K80kdump            S12rsyslog           S28autofs
K02oddjobd        K84wpa_supplicant   S13cpuspeed          S30vboxadd
K05wdaemon        K86cgred            S13irqbalance        S30vboxadd-x11
K10psacct         K87restorecond      S13rpcbind           S35vboxadd-service
K10saslauthd      K88sssd             S15mdmonitor         S50bluetooth
K15httpd          K89rdisc            S22messagebus        S55sshd
K50dnsmasq        K95cgconfig         S23NetworkManager    S70spice-vdagentd
K50netconsole     K95firstboot        S24avahi-daemon      S80postfix
K50snmpd          K99rngd             S24nfslock           S82abrt-ccpp
K50snmptrapd      S01sysstat          S24rpcgssd           S82abrtd
K60nfs            S02lvm2-monitor     S24rpcidmapd         S82abrt-oops
K69rpcsvcgssd     S08ip6tables        S25cups              S90crond
K73ypbind         S08iptables         S25netfs             S95atd
K74ntpd           S10network          S26acpid             S97rhnsd
K75ntpdate        S11auditd           S26haldaemon         S99certmonger
K75quota_nld      S11portreserve      S26udev-post         S99local
```

Oracle Linux System Configuration and Process Management

Describe the /etc/sysconfig directory

The /etc/sysconfig/ directory contains a variety of Linux system configuration files. The specific files vary depending on what packages have been installed on your system. A sample listing from the /etc/sysconfig directory of an Oracle Linux 6 system is shown below. The contents of your own /etc/sysconfig directory may be different.

```
[root@matthew sysconfig]# ls
atd          init               network-scripts   saslauthd
auditd       ip6tables          nfs               selinux
authconfig   ip6tables-config   nspluginwrapper   smartmontools
autofs       ip6tables.old      ntpd              snmpd
cbq          iptables           ntpdate           snmptrapd
cgconfig     iptables-config    prelink           sshd
cgred.conf   iptables.old       quota_nld         sysstat
clock        irqbalance         raid-check        sysstat.ioconf
console      kdump              readahead         system-config-firewall
cpuspeed     kernel             readonly-root     system-config-firewall.old
crond        keyboard           rhn               system-config-users
firstboot    modules            rngd              udev
grub         netconsole         rsyslog           wpa_supplicant
httpd        network            samba
i18n         networking         sandbox
```

Some of the files in the sysconfig directory and their purpose are:

- **authconfig** -- Sets the authorization to be used on the host.
- **autofs** -- Defines custom options for the automatic mounting of devices.
- **clock** -- Controls the interpretation of values read from the system hardware clock.
- **desktop** -- Specifies the desktop for new users and the display manager to run when entering runlevel 5.
- **dhcpd** -- Used to pass arguments to the dhcpd daemon.
- **firstboot** -- Defines whether to run the firstboot utility.
- **init** -- Controls how the system appears and functions during the boot process.

- **iptables-config** -- Stores information used by the kernel to set up packet filtering services at boot time or whenever the service is started.
- **keyboard** -- Controls the behavior of the keyboard.
- **network** -- Used to specify information about the desired network configuration.
- **networkscripts** -- Directory of configuration files for network interfaces.
- **ntpd** -- Used to pass arguments to the ntpd daemon at boot time.
- **samba** -- Used to pass arguments to the smbd and the nmbd daemons at boot time.
- **selinux** -- Contains the basic configuration options for SELinux.
- **system-config-users** -- The configuration file for the graphical application, User Manager.

Examine the /proc file system

The /proc/ directory in Linux (sometimes referred to as the proc file system) is a pseudo-file system which is used as an interface to kernel data structures. The files represent the current state of the kernel. This allows user and applications to access the kernel's view of the system. The files in the directory contain information about system hardware and all running processes. While most are read-only, some of the files within the /proc/ directory can be manipulated to make configuration changes to the kernel.

The /proc/ directory contains virtual files and is often referred to as a virtual file system. Most of the virtual files are listed as being zero bytes in size. However, they can still contain a large amount of information when viewed. Most of the time and date stamps on the /proc virtual files show the current time and date. This is because they are constantly being updated. Some of the common subdirectories and their contents are listed below:

- **/proc/[pid]** -- Numerical subdirectory for each process on system
- **/proc/[pid]/limits** -- Displays the soft limit, hard limit, and units of measurement for each of the process's resource limits
- **/proc/bus** -- Contains subdirectories for installed busses
- **/proc/cmdline** -- Arguments passed to the Linux kernel at boot time
- **/proc/cpuinfo** -- Contains CPU information
- **/proc/diskstats** -- Contains disk I/O statistics for each disk device
- **/proc/filesystems** -- Listing of file systems supported by the kernel
- **/proc/loadavg** -- Load average information
- **/proc/meminfo** -- Statistics about the memory usage on the system
- **/proc/modules** -- Kernel modules (or use 'lsmod' command to list loaded kernel modules)
- **/proc/net** -- Various net pseudo-files, all of which give the status of some part of the networking layer
- **/proc/stat** -- Kernel/system statistics
- **/proc/swaps** -- Information about swap usage
- **/proc/sys** -- Contains a number of files/subdirectories corresponding to kernel variables
- **/proc/uptime** -- Contains uptime in seconds and total time(seconds) spent in idle process
- **/proc/version** -- Version of the Linux kernel
- **/proc/vmstat** -- Virtual memory statistics

Describe the sysfs file system

Similar to /proc, the sysfs is a virtual filesystem used by the kernel to represent kernel objects, their attributes, and their relationships with each other. The sysfs file system is mounted at /sys and contains subdirectories organized in a hierarchical structure. When sysfs was added to Linux, it allowed much of the hardware information that had previously been located in /proc to be relocated. The result is a cleaner interface in the /proc filesystem. Programs such as udev use the sysfs file system to access device and device driver information.

The organization of the sysfs directory hierarchy is based the internal organization of kernel data structures. They are mostly ASCII files and usually contain one value each. This makes the exported information accurate and easily accessible. The top level of the sysfs mount point contains a number of directories. These represent the major subsystems that are registered with sysfs. The directories are generated at system startup when the subsystems register themselves with the kobject core. Once initialized, they can begin to discover objects, which are then placed within their respective directories. The top level of the Oracle Linux 6 /sys directory looks like the following:

```
[root@matthew sys]# ls -l
total 0
drwxr-xr-x. 2 root root 0 Sep 15 11:41 block
drwxr-xr-x. 19 root root 0 Sep 15 11:41 bus
drwxr-xr-x. 42 root root 0 Sep 15 11:41 class
drwxr-xr-x. 4 root root 0 Sep 15 11:41 dev
drwxr-xr-x. 12 root root 0 Sep 15 11:41 devices
drwxr-xr-x. 4 root root 0 Sep 15 11:41 firmware
drwxr-xr-x. 6 root root 0 Sep 15 11:41 fs
drwxr-xr-x. 2 root root 0 Sep 15 19:05 hypervisor
drwxr-xr-x. 5 root root 0 Sep 15 11:41 kernel
drwxr-xr-x. 108 root root 0 Sep 15 11:41 module
drwxr-xr-x. 2 root root 0 Sep 15 11:41 power
```

No files exist in this directory. Changing to the devices subdirectory and generating a directory listing gives the following results:

```
[root@matthew bus]# cd ./devices
[root@matthew devices]# ls -l
total 0
drwxr-xr-x. 3 root root 0 Sep 15 11:41 breakpoint
drwxr-xr-x. 8 root root 0 Sep 15 11:41 LNXSYSTM:00
drwxr-xr-x. 15 root root 0 Sep 15 11:41 pci0000:00
drwxr-xr-x. 11 root root 0 Sep 15 11:41 platform
drwxr-xr-x. 8 root root 0 Sep 15 11:41 pnp0
drwxr-xr-x. 3 root root 0 Sep 15 19:07 rapidio
drwxr-xr-x. 3 root root 0 Sep 15 11:41 software
drwxr-xr-x. 7 root root 0 Sep 15 11:41 system
drwxr-xr-x. 3 root root 0 Sep 15 11:41 tracepoint
drwxr-xr-x. 20 root root 0 Sep 15 11:41 virtual
```

No files exist in this directory. Changing to the system subdirectory and generating a directory listing gives the following results:

```
[root@matthew software]# cd ./system
[root@matthew system]# ls -l
total 0
drwxr-xr-x. 3 root root 0 Sep 15 19:25 clocksource
drwxr-xr-x. 5 root root 0 Sep 15 11:41 cpu
drwxr-xr-x. 3 root root 0 Sep 15 19:25 machinecheck
drwxr-xr-x. 10 root root 0 Sep 15 19:25 memory
drwxr-xr-x. 3 root root 0 Sep 15 19:25 node
```

No files exist in this directory. Changing to the cpu subdirectory and generating a directory listing gives the following results:

```
[root@matthew system]# cd ./cpu
[root@matthew cpu]# ls -l
total 0
drwxr-xr-x. 5 root root    0 Sep 15 11:41 cpu0
drwxr-xr-x. 2 root root    0 Sep 15 19:26 cpufreq
drwxr-xr-x. 2 root root    0 Sep 15 19:26 cpuidle
-r--r--r--. 1 root root 4096 Sep 15 19:26 kernel_max
-r--r--r--. 1 root root 4096 Sep 15 19:26 offline
-r--r--r--. 1 root root 4096 Sep 15 19:26 online
-r--r--r--. 1 root root 4096 Sep 15 19:26 possible
-r--r--r--. 1 root root 4096 Sep 15 19:26 present
--w-------. 1 root root 4096 Sep 15 19:26 probe
--w-------. 1 root root 4096 Sep 15 19:26 release
```

Finally at this level we have four readable files and two writeable ones. Looking at the readble files provides the following results:

```
[root@matthew cpu]# cat kernel_max
4095
[root@matthew cpu]# cat offline

[root@matthew cpu]# cat online
0
[root@matthew cpu]# cat possible
0
[root@matthew cpu]# cat present
0
```

As noted earlier, each file has a single value. This is an excellent design for programs that are trying to get information from this filesystem and very much a pain for humans trying to get information from it. The sysfs filesystem is not something designed for humans to poke around through multiple directories to get information one little piece at a time.

Use the sysctl utility

The sysctl utility allows you to display and change the current values of kernel parameters at runtime. The parameters accessible to sysctl are those listed under /proc/sys/. Some of the options of sysctl include:

- **-a** -- Display all values currently available for configuration/display.
- **-p** -- Load in sysctl settings from the file specified or /etc/sysctl.conf if no filename is supplied
- **-w** -- Use this option when you want to change a sysctl setting.

A partial listing from a sysctl -a follows:

```
[root@matthew cpu]# sysctl -a | less
kernel.sched_child_runs_first = 0
kernel.sched_min_granularity_ns = 750000
kernel.sched_latency_ns = 6000000
kernel.sched_wakeup_granularity_ns = 1000000
kernel.sched_tunable_scaling = 1
kernel.sched_migration_cost = 500000
kernel.sched_nr_migrate = 32
kernel.sched_time_avg = 1000
kernel.sched_shares_window = 10000000
kernel.timer_migration = 1
kernel.sched_rt_period_us = 1000000
kernel.sched_rt_runtime_us = 950000
kernel.panic = 0
kernel.core_uses_pid = 1
kernel.core_pipe_limit = 4
kernel.tainted = 0
kernel.latencytop = 0
kernel.real-root-dev = 0
kernel.print-fatal-signals = 0
...
```

Display and change the current values of kernel parameters using sysctl

You can view the values of individual kernel parameter by executing sysctl [parameter]. The following command displays the value of the kernel.hostname parameter:

```
[root@matthew cpu]# sysctl kernel.hostname
kernel.hostname = matthew.example.com
```

You can suppress the display of the kernel parameter name itself by using the -n option of sysctl:

```
[root@matthew cpu]# sysctl -n kernel.hostname
matthew.example.com
```

To change the values of kernel parameters with sysctl, you must use the -w option and supply the parameter and the intended value. First check out the value of the parameter to be changed. For this example, the net.ipv4.ip_forward kernel parameter is used:

```
[root@matthew cpu]# sysctl -n net.ipv4.ip_forward
0
```

The value is currently set to zero, which means IP forwarding is not enabled. The following command will enable it by setting thekernel parameter to 1:

```
[root@matthew cpu]# sysctl -w net.ipv4.ip_forward=1
net.ipv4.ip_forward = 1
```

Checking the parameter value again, we can see that the value has changed:

```
[root@matthew cpu]# sysctl -n net.ipv4.ip_forward
1
```

While the kernel parameter value has been changed, the new setting will not persist on reboot. In order to make persistent changes to kernel parameters, it is necessary to edit the parameter value in the /etc/sysctl.conf file. On system startup, the init program runs the /etc/rc.d/rc.sysinit script. This script contains a command that executes sysctl. The /etc/sysctl.conf file is used as the source of the values passed to the kernel. The values stored in this file will take effect each time the system boots. The following is a section of the /etc/sysctl.conf file. Since net.ipv4.ip_forward is the first parameter in the file, it is easy to see that the persistent setting is set to zero. In order to make the IPV4 IP Packet forwarding permanent, the file would be opened with vi (or another editor) and the value set to 1).

```
# Kernel sysctl configuration file for Red Hat Linux
#
# For binary values, 0 is disabled, 1 is enabled. See sysctl(8) and
# sysctl.conf(5) for more details.

# Controls IP packet forwarding
net.ipv4.ip_forward = 0

# Controls source route verification
net.ipv4.conf.default.rp_filter = 1

# Do not accept source routing
net.ipv4.conf.default.accept_source_route = 0

# Controls the System Request debugging functionality of the kernel
kernel.sysrq = 0

# Controls whether core dumps will append the PID to the core
filename.
# Useful for debugging multi-threaded applications.
kernel.core_uses_pid = 1
...
```

Use the ulimit command and the set parameters

Processes started from a shell in Linux obtain the resources available to that shell. Most Linux shells, like bash, provide control over those resources. You can set limits for processes started in the shell such as the maximum allowed open file descriptors or the maximum number of processes available. The ulimit command provides the means to view and set those limits. Executing ulimit -a will display all of the resources and limits on your current shell:

```
[root@matthew /]# ulimit -a
core file size          (blocks, -c) 0
data seg size           (kbytes, -d) unlimited
scheduling priority             (-e) 0
file size               (blocks, -f) unlimited
pending signals                 (-i) 7841
max locked memory       (kbytes, -l) 64
max memory size         (kbytes, -m) unlimited
open files                      (-n) 1024
pipe size            (512 bytes, -p) 8
POSIX message queues     (bytes, -q) 819200
real-time priority              (-r) 0
stack size              (kbytes, -s) 8192
cpu time               (seconds, -t) unlimited
max user processes              (-u) 1024
virtual memory          (kbytes, -v) unlimited
file locks                      (-x) unlimited
```

In the shell that generated those results, there is a limit is 1024 open files and 1024 user processes. When limits are set, they are categorized as either hard or soft. The -H and -S options of the ulimit command are used when setting limits to specify which type is being set. When a limit is soft, non root users can increase them with the ulimit command up to the maximum set by a hard limit. A hard limit cannot be increased by a non root user once it has been set. Some of the ulimit options include:

- **-a** -- All current limits are reported
- **-b** -- The maximum socket buffer size
- **-c** -- The maximum size of core files created
- **-d** -- The maximum size of a process's data segment
- **-e** -- The maximum scheduling priority ("nice")
- **-f** -- The maximum size of files written by the shell and its children
- **-i** -- The maximum number of pending signals
- **-l** -- The maximum size that may be locked into memory
- **-m** -- The maximum resident set size
- **-n** -- The maximum number of open file descriptors
- **-q** -- The maximum number of bytes in POSIX message queues

- **-r** -- The maximum real-time scheduling priority
- **-s** -- The maximum stack size
- **-u** -- The maximum number of processes available to a single user

If you want to check the max user processes limit, you can run the 'ulimit –u' command as shown below.

```
[root@matthew /]# ulimit -u
1024
```

The below example uses the ulimit command to change the max user processes limit. A value is supplied with the ulimit -u command to set the value. Then the ulimit -u command is used again to check that the value has been changed.

```
[root@matthew /]# ulimit -u 1090
[root@matthew /]# ulimit -u
1090
```

You can check hard limit of max user processes using the –H option of the ulimit command and the soft limit using the -S option. From the below, we can see that both are currently the same:

```
[root@matthew /]# ulimit -H -u
1090
[root@matthew /]# ulimit -S -u
1090
```

If the soft limit is set to a lower value, then a different value will be returned. Also, when neither hard nor soft is specified, the ulimit - u command returns the soft limit.

```
[root@matthew /]# ulimit -S -u 1000
[root@matthew /]# ulimit -u
1000
[root@matthew /]# ulimit -H -u
1090
[root@matthew /]# ulimit -S -u
1000
```

The /etc/security/limits.conf file is where the hard and soft limits for various resources can be set. A partial listing of that file is shown below. The file on your own system may be different.

```
# /etc/security/limits.conf
#
#Each line describes a limit for a user in the form:
#
#<domain>        <type>  <item>  <value>
#
#Where:
#<domain> can be:
#        - an user name
#        - a group name, with @group syntax
#        - the wildcard *, for default entry
#        - the wildcard %, can be also used with %group syntax,
#                 for maxlogin limit
#
#<type> can have the two values:
#        - "soft" for enforcing the soft limits
#        - "hard" for enforcing hard limits
#
#<item> can be one of the following:
#        - core - limits the core file size (KB)
#        - data - max data size (KB)
...
#
#<domain>      <type>  <item>         <value>
#
#*               soft    core            0
#*               hard    rss             10000
#@student        hard    nproc           20
#@faculty        soft    nproc           20
#@faculty        hard    nproc           50
#ftp             hard    nproc           0
#@student        -       maxlogins       4
# End of file
```

Find and control running programs with ps, top, kill, and nice

PS

The ps command displays a snapshot of information about active processes running on the system. By default, ps displays all processes with the same effective user ID as the current user and associated with the same terminal as the invoker. The default data shown are the process ID, the terminal associated with the process, the cumulated CPU time in [dd-]hh:mm:ss format, and the executable name. An example of this is below:

```
[root@matthew /]# ps
  PID TTY          TIME CMD
 2716 pts/0    00:00:00 bash
 3931 pts/0    00:00:00 ps
```

That aside, the ps command is seldom executed with the default options. The ps command contains a huge number of possible options (largely because it can be run using UNIX, BSD, or GNU option syntax). Run 'man ps' command if you are interested in what they are and how to use them. Everyone has their favorite ps options. Most of the time, I execute ps with the e (Select all processes) and f (Full-format listing) options. Since the listing of all processes can be very long, generally I pipe the output through grep to search for a particular string. An example of using ps to look for all processes running the bash shell follows:

```
[root@matthew /]# ps -ef | grep bash
root      2716  2714  0 16:44 pts/0    00:00:00 bash
root      3952  2716  0 22:46 pts/0    00:00:00 grep bash
```

The command picked up the one bash shell being run by the root user. The second line is the grep process that ps was using to look for the bash string. Notice that the results also include several columns not included in the first example. The leftmost column is the login id of the user that owns the process. The second column is the process id of the process. The third column is the parent process id of the process. Note that for the grep process line, its parent is the bash shell process. You can use the parent ids to track back through processes to determine the hierarchy. Running the ps command looking for process 2714 (the parent of the bash shell process) shows that the owner of the bash shell is a gnome-terminal process.

```
[root@matthew /]# ps -ef | grep 2714
root       2714     1  0 16:44 ?        00:00:20 gnome-terminal
root       2715  2714  0 16:44 ?        00:00:00 gnome-pty-helper
root       2716  2714  0 16:44 pts/0    00:00:00 bash
root       3968  2716  0 22:53 pts/0    00:00:00 grep 2714
```

TOP

The top program displays a real-time view of a running system. By default, top runs continuously, refreshing every three seconds. System summary information is shown along with a list of tasks currently being managed by the Linux kernel. The specific summary information to be displayed and the types, order and size of the information displayed for running tasks can be configured by the user and made persistent across reboots. However, unlike ps, the top command is most commonly run with no parameters. A partial display from top follows:

```
top - 23:10:10 up  6:27,  2 users,  load average: 0.00, 0.01, 0.05
Tasks: 141 total,   1 running, 140 sleeping,   0 stopped,   0 zombie
Cpu(s):  1.0%us,  0.7%sy,  0.0%ni, 98.3%id,  0.0%wa,  0.0%hi,  0.0%si,  0.0%st
Mem:   1020876k total,   874720k used,   146156k free,    34356k buffers
Swap:  2064380k total,        0k used,  2064380k free,   562372k cached

  PID USER      PR  NI  VIRT  RES  SHR S %CPU %MEM    TIME+  COMMAND
 2146 root      20   0  129m  27m 8196 S  0.7  2.8   0:46.56 Xorg
 2714 root      20   0  282m  12m 9396 S  0.7  1.3   0:21.39 gnome-terminal
 2344 root      20   0  197m 1496  976 S  0.3  0.1   0:51.39 VBoxClient
 2414 root      20   0  316m  11m 8768 S  0.3  1.1   0:25.61 wnck-applet
 4043 root      20   0 15080 1136  844 R  0.3  0.1   0:00.76 top
    1 root      20   0 19400 1516 1212 S  0.0  0.1   0:01.48 init
    2 root      20   0     0    0    0 S  0.0  0.0   0:00.02 kthreadd
    3 root      20   0     0    0    0 S  0.0  0.0   0:00.16 ksoftirqd/0
```

Top can be made to display a wide range of different columns. However, the information for the columns in the above top listing is:

- **PID** -- The process ID of the task
- **USER** -- The process owner
- **PR** -- The priority of the task
- **NI** -- The nice value of the task
- **VIRT** -- The total amount of virtual memory used by the task
- **RES** -- The non-swapped physical memory a task has used
- **SHR** -- The amount of shared memory used by a task
- **S** -- The status of the task which can be one of:
  - ✓ **D** -- uninterruptible sleep
  - ✓ **R** -- running
  - ✓ **S** -- sleeping
  - ✓ **T** -- traced or stopped
  - ✓ **Z** -- zombie
- **%CPU** -- The task's share of the elapsed CPU time since the last screen update, expressed as a percentage of total CPU time
- **%MEM** -- A task's currently used share of available physical memory
- **TIME+** -- CPU time to a granularity of hundredths of a second
- **COMMAND** -- The command line used to start a task or the name of the associated program

Top is commonly used to locate processes that are using excessive system resources. It is often an early step in diagnosing Linux sever performance problems. For example, a task might get hung while grabbing a significant amount of the CPU percentage. Using top is an easy way to locate such runaway processes. If required, you can use the kill command (described next) to end them.

KILL

The kill command sends a specified signal to a given process or process group. As the name suggests, that signal is most commonly used to kill the process. Once a process has been identified that you want to terminate (often using ps or top) you can use this command to terminate it. If process to be killed has the id 1000, the two common forms for ending the process are:

```
kill 1000
kill -9 1000
```

The first version will send a TERM signal to process 100. This is the preferred option as it asks the process to shut itself down in the hope that it can do so cleanly. Using the -9 option is more aggressive and sends a KILL signal. The kill signal forces the process to shut down without allowing it to do so itself. As a general rule, you should only use the KILL signal if killing the process with the TERM signal does not succeed.

Nice

Nice allows you to run a command with an adjusted niceness. Niceness affects how the kernel determines process scheduling. The kernel decides how much processor time is required for a process based on the nice value. Nicenesses range from -20 (most favorable scheduling) to 19 (least favorable).

Locating niceness levels in one of the times that the -ef options of ps are not sufficient (niceness is not one of the columns displayed). Using ps -ely will show the niceness of all running processes on your Linux system. The seventh column 'NI' is the niceness level.

```
[root@matthew /]# ps -ely
S   UID   PID  PPID  C PRI  NI   RSS    SZ WCHAN  TTY          TIME CMD
S     0     1     0  0  80   0  1516  4850 poll_s ?        00:00:01 init
S     0     2     0  0  80   0     0     0 kthrea ?        00:00:00 kthreadd
S     0     3     2  0  80   0     0     0 run_ks ?        00:00:00 ksoftirqd/0
S     0     6     2  0 -40   -     0     0 cpu_st ?        00:00:00 migration/0
S     0     7     2  0 -40   -     0     0 watchd ?        00:00:00 watchdog/0
S     0     8     2  0  60 -20     0     0 rescue ?        00:00:00 cpuset
S     0     9     2  0  60 -20     0     0 rescue ?        00:00:00 khelper
S     0    10     2  0  60 -20     0     0 rescue ?        00:00:00 netns
S     0    11     2  0  80   0     0     0 bdi_sy ?        00:00:00 sync_supers
S     0    12     2  0  80   0     0     0 bdi_fo ?        00:00:00 bdi-default
```

The nice command is used to start a process with a different niceness level. If the gedit program is started from the command line by itself, we can verify that the niceness value for it is zero (the default):

```
[root@matthew /]# gedit &
[1] 4355
[root@matthew /]# ps -ely | grep gedit
S     0  4355  2716  1  80   0 15680 76138 poll_s pts/0    00:00:00
gedit
```

After terminating the gedit process and starting it a second time using the nice command to set the niceness to 10, the ps shows a nice level of 10.

```
[root@matthew /]# nice -10 gedit &
[1]   Done                    gedit
[root@matthew /]# ps -ely | grep gedit
S     0  4370  2716  3  90  10 15720 76156 poll_s pts/0    00:00:00
gedit
```

While regular users can start processes with positive (lower priority) niceness levels, only root can start processes with negative niceness levels. Regular users will simply get an error message if they attempt to do so.

Use the jobs, fg and bg commands to view and access several tasks

The jobs command lists the jobs that are running in the background and in the foreground. If no jobs are present, then the prompt will be returned with no information. The jobs command has the following options:

- **-l** -- List process IDs in addition to the normal information.
- **-p** -- List only the process ID of the job's process group leader.
- **-n** -- Display information only about jobs that have changed status since the user was last notified.
- **-r** -- Restrict output to running jobs.
- **-s** -- Restrict output to stopped jobs.

Executing the jobs command shows the gedit process that was started earlier for the nice example.

```
[root@matthew /]# jobs
[2]+  Running                  nice -10 gedit &
```

The below example demonstrates the result of executing jobs with several of the options. The first line provides the process. The second line restricts to only running processes the third to stopped processes. Since the gedit process is running, the stopped filter generates no results.

```
[root@matthew /]# jobs -l
[2]+  4370 Running                  nice -10 gedit &
[root@matthew /]# jobs -lr
[2]+  4370 Running                  nice -10 gedit &
[root@matthew /]# jobs -ls
[root@matthew /]#
```

The reason why gedit shows up in the jobs output is because it had been started as a background process. The trailing ampersand (&) used in when executing gedit in the previous chapter forces the process to be run in the background rather than the foreground. Had gedit been started as a foreground process, the command prompt would not have come back to the terminal until gedit was terminated -- and it would not have been possible to run ps (from that terminal) and see the process. I could have opened a second terminal process while the first was dedicated to gedit, but running a gedit process in the background made more sense.

The bg command allows you to move a process into the background after it is already running. Had gedit been run without the trailing ampersand, bg could have been used to recover the command prompt without terminating gedit. To place a foreground process in the background: suspend the foreground process (with Ctrl-z) then enter the bg command to move the process into the background. To demonstrate, the gnome calculator (gcalctool) is run from a terminal session without a trailing ampersand. The screenshot below shows that the terminal prompt has not come back. The calculator process is running in the foreground:

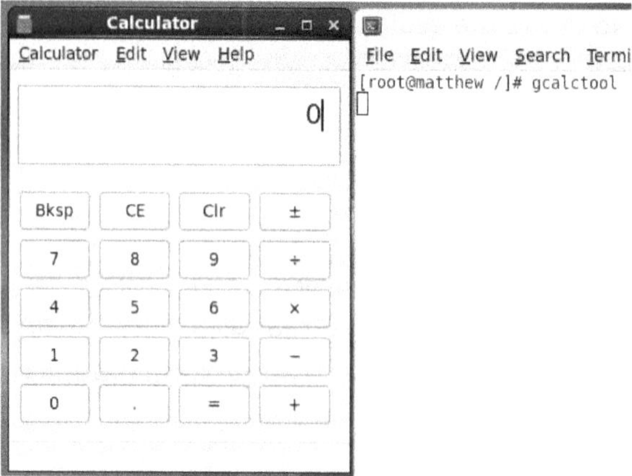

To move it to the background, the process is stopped by pressing Ctrl-Z.

```
[root@matthew /]# gcalctool
^Z
[3]+  Stopped                 gcalctool
```

Running the jobs command at this point shows two processes. In addition, running jobs with the -ls option returns results now since a stopped job exists.

```
[root@matthew /]# jobs
[2]-  Running                 nice -10 gedit &
[3]+  Stopped                 gcalctool
[root@matthew /]# jobs -ls
[3]+  4774 Stopped                 gcalctool
```

The stopped process can be restarted in the background by using the bg command. Running the jobs command again shows both background processes with a 'running' status:

```
[root@matthew /]# bg
[3]+ gcalctool &
[root@matthew /]# jobs
[2]-  Running                 nice -10 gedit &
[3]+  Running                 gcalctool &
```

The fg command pulls a job from the background into the foreground and makes it the current job. Running fg on the terminal pulls the gcalctool process back into the foreground (and hangs the terminal prompt again).

```
[root@matthew /]# fg
gcalctool
```

Executing fg with no parameter allowed Linux to determine which background process to bring back to the foreground. If the intent had been to bring the gedit process back to the foreground, the output from the jobs command comes into play. The background processes displayed in jobs were numbered. Supplying that number to fg will bring a specific job back into the foreground. In the below example, the gcalctool process is stopped and moved to the background again. Then jobs is run to get the job ID numbers of the two processes. Finally, he gedit process is brought back into the foreground by using the job number:

```
[root@matthew /]# fg
gcalctool
^Z
[3]+  Stopped                  gcalctool
[root@matthew /]# bg
[3]+ gcalctool &
[root@matthew /]# jobs
[2]-  Running                  nice -10 gedit &
[3]+  Running                  gcalctool &
[root@matthew /]# fg %2
nice -10 gedit
```

If you log out of Linux while jobs that you started are running in the background, they will be terminated. If the process should continue to run after you log out, it is possible to use the disown command to remove ownership of it before logging out.

Oracle Linux Package Management

Describe Oracle Linux package management

Oracle Linux package management is essentially Red Hat package management. The two tools used by Oracle Linux to manage packages are the Red Hat Package Manager and Yum (Yellowdog Updater, Modified). It is also possible to install packages manually using tarballs, but that is becoming less common and is not likely to be something you will see on the exam (nor is it technically package management).

RPM

The RPM Package Manager (RPM) is an open packaging system, which runs on Oracle Linux, Red Hat Enterprise Linux and several other Linux distributions. The utility was created by Red Hat, but they encourage other vendors to use RPM for their own products (CentOS, Fedora, and SUSE all use it). RPM is free software package released under the GNU License. The utility works only with packages specifically built for processing by the rpm package. RPM can install, uninstall, and upgrade RPM packages with short commands. RPM maintains a database of installed packages and their files and allows you to perform queries and verifications on the packages installed on your system.

YUM

Yum is a utility built on top of the RPM infrastructure. It can automatically update, install, or remove packages in rpm systems. Yum will automatically compute dependencies and determine what actions are required to install packages. Yum has a plugin interface for adding simple features and can also be used from other python programs via its module inteface. Yum can interface with Oracle's public Yum server and also with the ULN server to obtain packages, patches, and updates.

Use the RPM utility

An RPM file, also known as a package, is a way of distributing software so that it can be easily installed, upgraded, queried, and deleted. RPM files contain information such as the package name, version, other file dependency information, and platform. They also contain meta-data used to install and erase the archive files. The meta-data includes helper scripts, file attributes, and descriptive information about the package.

Some of the common options used with the rpm command are:

- **i** -- Install package
- **U** -- Upgrade package
- **e** -- Erase/remove package
- **F** -- Freshen package
- **q** -- Query option
- **V** -- Verify option
- **h** -- Print 50 hash marks as the package archive is unpacked.
- **v** -- Print verbose information.

Install

As a general rule, RPM packages have file names like pkgname-1.0-1.i386.rpm. The file name includes the package name (pkgname), version (1.0), release (1), and architecture (i386). To install a package using RPM, log in as root and type the following command at a shell prompt:

```
rpm -ivh pkgname-1.0-1.i386.rpm
```

Uninstall

To uninstall a package with RPM utility, type the following command at a shell prompt:

```
rpm -e pkgname
```

Upgrade

When upgrading a package, RPM will automatically uninstall any old versions of the package. The Upgrade option will install a package even if there are no previous versions of the package installed. Type the following command at a shell prompt:

```
rpm -Uvh pkgname-2.0-1.i386.rpm
```

Freshen

Freshening is similar to upgrading, except that only existent packages are upgraded. The RPM utility will check the versions of the packages specified against the versions of packages that have already been installed on your system. When a newer version of an already-installed package is processed by RPM's freshen option, it is upgraded to the newer version. Type the following command at a shell prompt:

```
rpm -Fvh pkgname-2.0-1.i386.rpm
```

Verify

Verifying a package compares information about files installed from a package with the same information from the original package. Among other things, verifying compares the size, MD5 sum, permissions, type, owner, and group of each file. This is useful if you suspect that your RPM databases are corrupt. If everything verified properly, there is no output. If there are any discrepancies, they are displayed. It is possible to verify a complete package, a single file, or all packages in your system (among other options).

To verify a single package:

```
rpm -V pkgname
```

To verify a package containing a particular file:

```
rpm -Vf /usr/bin/[filename]
```

To verify ALL installed packages throughout the system:

```
rpm -Va
```

Describe the Oracle Public YUM Server

Oracle's public Yum server is a site containing software for Oracle Linux and Oracle VM. The yum server offers a free method for installing packages from Oracle Linux and Oracle VM installation media via a yum client. It requires no subscription and can be used to obtain all errata and updates for Oracle Linux. The public yum server, like ULN, contains updates to the base distribution. However, unlike ULN, it does not include Oracle-specific software.

By default, Oracle Linux 6 is configured to use the Oracle public yum repository. However, if there were some reason that a server were not configured properly, or the file was accidentally removed, this is how you would get the required .repo file. To download the Oracle public yum repository configuration file, as root, change directory to /etc/yum.repos.d:

```
cd /etc/yum.repos.d
```

Use the wget utility to download the repository configuration file that is appropriate for your system. For Oracle Linux 6, enter:

```
wget http://public-yum.oracle.com/public-yum-ol6.repo
```

The /etc/yum.repos.d directory is updated with the repository configuration file, in this example, public-yum-ol6.repo. You can enable or disable repositories in the public-yum-ol6.repo file by setting the value of the enabled directive to 1 or 0 as required.

When Oracle Linux is configured to use the public Yum server, running 'yum update' will allow you to obtain any relevant security or bugfix errata for Oracle Linux 6 posted to the public yum server.

Describe and configure YUM repositories

A package repository used by yum is directory that contains one or more RPMs plus some meta information. The meta information is used by yum so that it can determine details such as dependencies and file lists regarding the RPMs. Once the repository has been configured, yum can access this directory over ftp/http or a file URI. One possible yum repository is the Oracle public yum server. Another is the Unbreakable Linux Network site.

Repository configuration files are used to provide Yum with the information needed to access a given repository. These files are stored in the /etc/yum.repos.d/ directory. Checking that directory, there is a single file for the Oracle Public yum server (as mentioned in the previous section).

```
[root@matthew yum.repos.d]# ls -l
total 4
-rw-r--r--. 1 root root 2778 Sep 10 19:33 public-yum-ol6.repo
```

The repository file contains information for a number of individual repositories at public-yum.oracle.com. A partial listing is shown below:

```
[ol6_latest]
name=Oracle Linux $releasever Latest ($basearch)
baseurl=http://public-yum.oracle.com/repo/OracleLinux/OL6/latest/$basearch/
gpgkey=file:///etc/pki/rpm-gpg/RPM-GPG-KEY-oracle
gpgcheck=1
enabled=1

[ol6_addons]
name=Oracle Linux $releasever Add ons ($basearch)
baseurl=http://public-yum.oracle.com/repo/OracleLinux/OL6/addons/$basearch/
gpgkey=file:///etc/pki/rpm-gpg/RPM-GPG-KEY-oracle
gpgcheck=1
enabled=0

[ol6_ga_base]
name=Oracle Linux $releasever GA installation media copy ($basearch)
baseurl=http://public-yum.oracle.com/repo/OracleLinux/OL6/0/base/$basearch/
gpgkey=file:///etc/pki/rpm-gpg/RPM-GPG-KEY-oracle
gpgcheck=1
enabled=0

[ol6_u1_base]
name=Oracle Linux $releasever Update 1 installation media copy ($basearch)
baseurl=http://public-yum.oracle.com/repo/OracleLinux/OL6/1/base/$basearch/
gpgkey=file:///etc/pki/rpm-gpg/RPM-GPG-KEY-oracle
gpgcheck=1
enabled=0
```

Most of the repositories have the enabled flag set to zero, which means they are disabled and not available to yum. Each repository has a different purpose. For example ol6_latest has the latest versions of all packages, regardless of the specific Oracle Linux release they belong to. By contrast the ol6_u1_base repository will only have the latest versions of packages associated with Linux 6 Update 1. You must understand what a given repository is for before enabling or disabling access to it.

Use the YUM utility

The Yum utility has a dizzying number of potential options. The most commonly used yum commands are listed below:

- **install** -- Will install the latest version of a package or group of packages while ensuring that all dependencies are satisfied.
- **update** -- If run without supplying a package name, this will update every currently installed package. If one or more packages or package globs are specified, Yum will only update the listed packages. While updating packages, yum will ensure that all dependencies are satisfied.

- **remove** or **erase** -- Either command will remove the specified packages from the system as well as removing any packages which depend on the one being removed.
- **list** -- Lists various information about available packages.
- **search** -- This is used to find packages when you know something about the package but are not sure of its name. By default search looks at just package names and summaries. If that fails to return results, it will then try descriptions and url.
- **repolist** -- Produces a list of configured repositories. The default is to list all enabled repositories.

For an example, let us look for a text editor to replace vi. Some people swear by emacs, so we can use yum to search for it.

```
[root@matthew yum.repos.d]# yum search emacs
Loaded plugins: refresh-packagekit, security
================================ N/S Matched: emacs ================================
emacs.x86_64 : GNU Emacs text editor
emacs-a2ps.x86_64 : Emacs bindings for a2ps files
emacs-a2ps-el.x86_64 : Elisp source files for emacs-a2ps under GNU Emacs
emacs-anthy.noarch : Compiled elisp files to run Anthy under GNU Emacs
emacs-anthy-el.noarch : Elisp source files for Anthy under GNU Emacs
emacs-auctex.noarch : Enhanced TeX modes for Emacs
emacs-auctex-el.noarch : Elisp source files for emacs-auctex
emacs-common.x86_64 : Emacs common files
emacs-el.x86_64 : Emacs Lisp source files included with Emacs.
emacs-git.noarch : Git version control system support for Emacs
emacs-git-el.noarch : Elisp source files for git version control system support for
                    : Emacs
emacs-gnuplot.x86_64 : Emacs bindings for the gnuplot main application
emacs-gnuplot-el.x86_64 : Emacs bindings for the gnuplot main application
emacs-mercurial.x86_64 : Mercurial version control system support for Emacs
emacs-mercurial-el.x86_64 : Elisp source files for mercurial under GNU Emacs
emacs-nox.x86_64 : GNU Emacs text editor without X support
emacs-pyrex.noarch : Pyrex editing mode for Emacs
ocaml-emacs.x86_64 : Emacs mode for Objective Caml
ctags-etags.x86_64 : Exuberant Ctags for emacs tag format
emacs-auctex-doc.noarch : Documentation in various formats for AUCTeX

  Name and summary matches only, use "search all" for everything.
[root@matthew yum.repos.d]#
```

The base editor is at the top of the list above. In the screenshot below, yum is used to install emacs. The dependencies checks have been removed from the screenshot below to reduce it to a manageable size. Once Yum locates the files and resolves the dependencies, it shows how large of a download is required plus the installed size and asks if you really want to install the package.

```
[root@matthew yum.repos.d]# yum install emacs.x86_64
Loaded plugins: refresh-packagekit, security
Setting up Install Process
Resolving Dependencies
--> Running transaction check
---> Package emacs.x86_64 1:23.1-21.el6_2.3 will be installed
--> Processing Dependency: emacs-common = 1:23.1-21.el6_2.3 for package: 1:emacs-23.1

--> Finished Dependency Resolution

Dependencies Resolved

==========================================================================================
 Package                Arch          Version                  Repository          Size
==========================================================================================
Installing:
 emacs                  x86_64        1:23.1-21.el6_2.3        ol6_latest         2.2 M
Installing for dependencies:
 emacs-common           x86_64        1:23.1-21.el6_2.3        ol6_latest          18 M
 libXaw                 x86_64        1.0.11-2.el6             ol6_latest         178 k
 libXpm                 x86_64        3.5.10-2.el6             ol6_latest          50 k
 libotf                 x86_64        0.9.9-3.1.el6            ol6_latest          79 k
 m17n-db-datafiles      noarch        1.5.5-1.1.el6            ol6_latest         717 k

Transaction Summary
==========================================================================================
Install       6 Package(s)

Total download size: 21 M
Installed size: 73 M
Is this ok [y/N]:
```

The Yum utility behavior is controlled by the information in the /etc/yum.conf file. This is an ASCII file and can be modified with any text editor. An example is shown below:

```
[main]
cachedir=/var/cache/yum/$basearch/$releasever
keepcache=0
debuglevel=2
logfile=/var/log/yum.log
exactarch=1
obsoletes=1
gpgcheck=1
plugins=1
installonly_limit=3
```

The options in the above portion of the yum.conf file are:

- **cachedir** -- The absolute path to the directory where Yum should store its cache and database files.

- **keepcache** -- Can be either 0 to clear the cache of headers and packages after a successful installation (the default), or 1 to retain the cache after a successful installation.
- **debuglevel** -- Can be an integer between 1 and 10. A higher debuglevel value causes yum to display more detailed debugging output. A level of 0 disables debugging output. The default is 2.
- **logfile** -- An absolute path to the file in which yum should write its logging output.
- **exactarch** -- Can be either 0 which does not take into account the exact architecture when updating packages or 1 where the exact architecture is considered when updating packages (the default).
- **obsoletes** -- Can be 0, which disables yum's obsoletes processing logic when performing updates or 1 that enables yum's obsoletes processing logic when performing updates (the default).
- **gpgcheck** -- Can be 0, which disables GPG signature-checking on packages in all repositories, or 1 that enables it (the default).
- **plugins** -- Can be 0, which disables all Yum plug-ins globally, or 1that enable all Yum plug-ins globally (the default).
- **installonly_limit** -- Is is an integer representing the maximum number of versions that can be installed simultaneously for any single package listed in the installonlypkgs directive.

Describe the Unbreakable Linux Network (ULN)

Oracle's Unbreakable Linux Network (ULN) is a subscription-based service that provides support similar to, but beyond that available at Oracle's Public YUM Server. It is available to companies with an Oracle Unbreakable Linux support subscription. The ULN contains updates, software patches, and fixes for Oracle Linux and Oracle VM. It has packages that are not included in the original distribution available for download. The site also has information on yum, Ksplice, and support policies. Periodically the ULN Alert Notification will determine if updates applicable to your system are available at ULN and notify you.

It is possible to use yum in conjunction with ULN to manage your Linux installation. The system must be registered with ULN and subscribed to one or more ULN channels. During the subscription process, the latest version is automatically selected based on the architecture and operating system revision of the system being registered. When Once the system is registered, yum is able to connect to the ULN repository and download the latest RPM packages. You can then choose which of the packages you wish to install on your system.

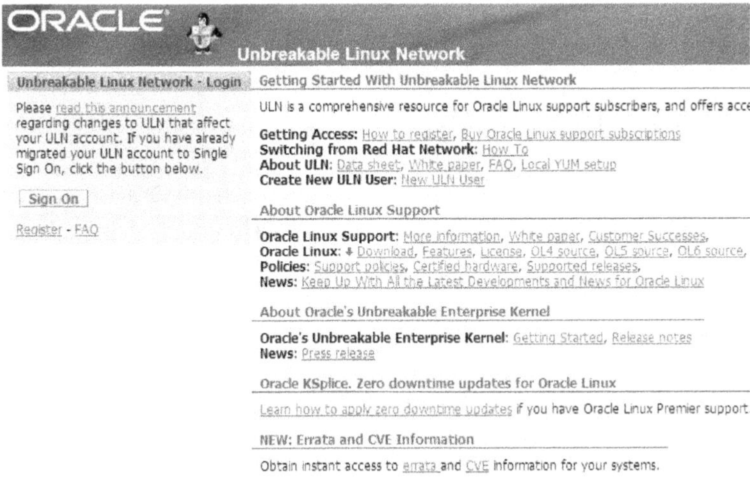

The packages available on ULN are available via channels. ULN channels exist for the i386, x86_64, and ia64 architectures, for releases of Oracle Linux 4 update 6 and later. There are also ULN channels for MySQL, Oracle VM, OCFS2, RDS, and productivity applications.

Systems are subscribed to the appropriate architecture and to the desired update level that is to be maintained. It is possible to maintain a specific OS revision or allow it to be updated with packages from later revisions. Some of the main channels available on ULN are:

- **_latest** -- Provides all the packages in a distribution, including any errata that are also provided in the patch channel. Unless you explicitly specify the version, any package that you download on this channel will be the most recent that is available.
- **_base** -- Provides the packages for each major version and minor update of Oracle Linux and Oracle VM. This channel corresponds

to the released ISO media image. Oracle does not publish security errata and bug fixes on these channels.

- **_patch** -- Provides only those packages that have changed since the initial release of a major or minor version of Oracle Linux or Oracle VM. The patch channel always provides the most recent version of a package, including all fixes that have been provided since the initial version was released.
- **_addons** -- Provides packages that are not included in the base distribution, such as the package that you can use to create a yum repository on Oracle Linux 6.
- **_oracle** -- Provides freely downloadable RPMs from Oracle that you can install on Oracle Linux, such as ASMLib and Oracle Instant Client.

Switch from Red Hat Network (RHN) to ULN

In order to switch from RHN to ULN, you must have an active ULN account. You can create a ULN account at http://linux.oracle.com/register.

To switch an Oracle Linux 6 system from RHN to ULN.

1. Run the uln_register command.

```
# uln_register
```

Alternatively, if you use the GNOME graphical user desktop, select System > Administration > ULN Registration. You can also register your system with ULN if you configure networking when installing Oracle Linux 6.

2. When prompted, enter your ULN user name, password, and customer support identifier (CSI).

3. Enter a name for the system that will allow you to identify it on ULN, and choose whether to upload hardware and software profile data that allows ULN to select the appropriate packages for the system.

4. If you have an Oracle Linux Premier Support account, you can choose to configure an Oracle Linux 6 system that is running a supported kernel to receive kernel updates from Oracle Ksplice.

To switch a Red Hat Enterprise Linux 6 system from RHN to ULN.

1. Download the uln_register.tgz package from http://linux-update.oracle.com/rpms to a temporary directory. If the rhn-setup-gnome package is already installed on your system, also download the uln_register-gnome.tgz from the same URL.

2. Extract the packages using the following command.

```
# tar -xzf uln_register.tgz
```

If the rhn-setup-gnome package is installed on your system, extract the packages from uln_register-gnome.tgz.

```
# tar -xzf uln_register-gnome.tgz
```

3. Change to the uln_migrate directory and install the registration packages.

```
# cd ./uln_migrate
# rpm -Uvh *.rpm
```

4. Run the uln_register command.

```
# uln_register
```

5. Follow the instructions on the screen to complete the registration. The uln_register utility collects information about your system and uploads it to Oracle.

Equivalent procedures for switching Red Hat Enterprise Linux 3, 4, and 5 from RHN to ULN are available at http://linux.oracle.com/switch.html

Install the Oracle RDBMS Server 11gR2 Pre-install RPM package for Oracle Linux 6

The Oracle RDBMS Server 11gR2 Pre-install RPM package makes it easier to install Oracle Database 11gR2. The package is available either from the Oracle Public Yum Server or the ULN network. The package name is "oracle-rdbms-server-11gR2-preinstall" (it was formerly known as "oracle-validated").

Before Oracle Database 11g R2 can be installed on Oracle Linux 6, there are several prerequisites outlined in the Linux Installation Guides that must be met. The pre-install RPM will perform most of the pre-installation configuration tasks for you. Among other things, the package creates the 'oracle' user and the groups needed for Oracle Database installation. It also modifies kernel parameters in /etc/sysctl.conf and resource limits in /etc/security/limits.conf. It also ensures that several packages required by Oracle are installed on the system. Using the yum info function provides the following data about the package:

```
[root@matthew yum.repos.d]# yum info oracle-rdbms-server-11gR2-
preinstall
Loaded plugins: refresh-packagekit, security
Available Packages
Name        : oracle-rdbms-server-11gR2-preinstall
Arch        : x86_64
Version     : 1.0
Release     : 7.el6
Size        : 15 k
Repo        : ol6_latest
Summary     : Sets the system for Oracle single instance and Real
            : Application Cluster install for Oracle Linux 6
License     : GPL
Description : This package installs software packages and sets
            : system parameters required for Oracle single instance
            : and Real Application Clusterinstall for Oracle Linux
            : Release 6 Files affected: /etc/sysctl.conf,
            : /etc/security/limits.conf, /boot/grub/menu.lst
```

The package is installed by issuing the command:

```
yum install oracle-rdbms-server-11gR2-preinstall
```

Once installed, the oracle user is created, as is the dba group:

```
[root@matthew yum.repos.d]# cat /etc/passwd | grep -i oracle
oracle:x:54321:54321::/home/oracle:/bin/bash
[root@matthew yum.repos.d]# cat /etc/group | grep -i oracle
dba:x:54322:oracle
```

Among the many changes made are a number of new settings in /etc/sysctl.conf:

```
# oracle-rdbms-server-11gR2-preinstall setting for fs.file-max is 6815744
fs.file-max = 6815744

# oracle-rdbms-server-11gR2-preinstall setting for kernel.sem is '250 32000 100 128'
kernel.sem = 250 32000 100 128

# oracle-rdbms-server-11gR2-preinstall setting for kernel.shmmni is 4096
kernel.shmmni = 4096

# oracle-rdbms-server-11gR2-preinstall setting for kernel.shmall is 1073741824 on x86
_64
# oracle-rdbms-server-11gR2-preinstall setting for kernel.shmall is 2097152 on i386
kernel.shmall = 1073741824
```

Set up a local YUM repository

Having a local YUM repository pointing to an ISO image or DVD with can be useful when you do not have an internet connection to access the Oracle Public Yum Server. If you are using Virtualbox and have an ISO image of the Oracle Linux 6 installation DVD, or if you have a physical DVD of it, then this can be used as a local yum repository.

In the example below, the Oracle Linux 6 installation DVD has been made available to Linux as /dev/sr0. The drive is then mounted in a newly created subdirectory called /mnt/OL6_LOCAL:

```
[root@matthew mnt]# mkdir OL6_LOCAL
[root@matthew mnt]# mount /dev/sr0 /mnt/OL6_LOCAL
mount: block device /dev/sr0 is write-protected, mounting read-only
```

The data is now available locally:

```
[root@matthew mnt]# cd OL6_LOCAL
[root@matthew OL6_LOCAL]# ls
EFI               isolinux          RELEASE-NOTES-en.html          RPM-GPG-KEY
EULA              LoadBalancer      RELEASE-NOTES-x86_64-en        RPM-GPG-KEY-oracle
eula.en_US        media.repo        RELEASE-NOTES-x86_64-en.html   ScalableFileSystem
eula.py           Packages          RELEASE-NOTES-x86-en           Server
GPL               README-en         RELEASE-NOTES-x86-en.html      supportinfo
HighAvailability  README-en.html    repodata                       TRANS.TBL
images            RELEASE-NOTES-en  ResilientStorage               UEK2
```

With the DVD mounted, it is now possible to create a repository configuration file that will allow it to be used as a yum repository. The configuration file is a text file that can be created with any editor. It requires only three lines. The information in the first two lines is largely arbitrary. Their purpose is just to name and describe the repository. The third line must properly refer to the directory where the DVD has been mounted.

```
[root@matthew ~]# cat /etc/yum.repos.d/local.repo
[local]
name=OL6 Local Repository
baseurl=file:///OL6_LOCAL
```

Once that file exists, yum can access it to pull packages from to be installed. As a general rule, this particular exercise is not something that you would do if your system has access to the internet. Pulling package information from the public yum server is much preferable to a local DVD as the packages will be more current.

Ksplice Zero Downtime Updates

Describe the purpose of Ksplice

About once a month, Linux kernel updates are released that contain important new security and reliability patches. Best practices, and in some cases industry regulations, require companies to apply these security updates and patches regularly. Failure to maintain a kernel with these updates can cause security to be compromised. However, most Kernel updates require a system reboot for them to become effective. For systems that are in 24x7 use, rebooting servers to apply these patches is both costly and disruptive.

Ksplice is a feature of Oracle Linux that enables important kernel patches and security updates to be applied without rebooting the system. With Ksplice Zero Downtime patching, it is possible to eliminate the downtime and disruption associated with installing and applying important kernel and security updates. It is possible to install a Ksplice delivered kernel patch while applications are running on your Oracle Linux 6 system. The Ksplice Zero downtime patching feature is part of the Oracle Linux Premier Support offering.

Describe the benefits of Ksplice

Using Ksplice provides several advantages over traditionally installed kernel updates. Some of the advantages are:

- **Reduce operational costs** -- On high availability systems, reboots need to be planned in advance, carefully schedules, and closely monitored. Complications can arise during a reboot causing downtime beyond the scheduled window. Services might not start properly when the system comes back up or the interruption may lead to complications with a separate system. Ksplice can eliminate long nights and weekends spent rebooting servers for kernel updates. It also eliminates the need to coordinate with system users about outages caused by reboots.

- **Improve availability** -- Updates installed using Ksplice are completed in a matter of seconds. Updates do not interrupt running applications or the people using those applications. Installing updates requires no downtime, so the system availability is increased. If there is a requirement to roll back an update for any reason, it is possible to do so easily, also without requiring a reboot.
- **Improve security** -- Systems that do not have the latest security patches in place are vulnerable to well-known security problems. Postponing the installation of updates until a reboot can occur without disrupting the business is a dangerous practice. Ksplice allows you to reduce the window of vulnerability by introducing updates more rapidly, allowing you to increase compliance with OS updates.
- **Improved support for Linux** -- Oracle Linux Premier Support customers get the benefit of using Ksplice for zero downtime diagnostic and security patches along with "Premier Backports". Premier Backports are fixes for the specific OS version being run, with no forced upgrades.

Describe how Ksplice works

Ksplice works by breaking the kernel into a sequence of security patches and bug fixes. There are versions of this 'broken out' kernel available for both the Unbreakable Enterprise Kernel and the Red Hat Compatible Kernel. When a new kernel update becomes available, client software on the system to be updated downloads the updates and applies them to the running kernel. Ksplice can operate in three different modes:

- **Standard** -- When the standard method is used, each system connects to the Oracle servers to download updates. Every system will need network access in order to use Ksplice. When running in this mode, Ksplice can work through proxies and firewalls, only one port and up to four IP addresses must be allowed. The Ksplice client running on each system will check with the Oracle servers approximately once every four hours to download updates. If any updates are located, they will be downloaded automatically. By default the updates will not be installed without user action. Configuring systems to automatically update is optional.

- **Local** -- The local method makes use of a Ksplice local server. In this method, each system connects only to a local system. That local system in turn is the only machine that will connect to the Oracle Ksplice servers. The Ksplice Local Server option requires the installation of additional software. Only the local Ksplice server requires network access. The local Ksplice server is much like a local yum repository and the setup and functionality is very similar.
- **Offline** -- When using the offline method, no connection to the Oracle Ksplice servers is required. When using this method, Ksplice updates are distributed using RPMs. The RPMs then must be installed on each Ksplice system -- usually through a local yum repository. The Ksplice command line client is still used to update the kernel.

As a rule of thumb, the standard version is recommended. It is fast and easy to install. Kernel updates are available automatically without any additional infrastructure. Connecting a system to access the Ksplice servers requires a minimal amount of network access and bandwidth costs are slight. The Local Server method makes sense if there is a requirement to minimize the number of outgoing connections. The offline method will work (indeed is the only possibility) for systems that have zero network access.

Configure and use Ksplice

There are three steps required to set up Ksplice:

- Get the Ksplice Uptrack access key (license key)
- Setup Oracle Ksplice Uptrack account
- Download and install Ksplice software

Ksplice is free for customers that have Oracle Linux Premier Support. Premier Support customers can get an access key by logging in to the

Unbreakable Linux Network and following the instructions to register their system for Ksplice. It is also possible to get a 30-day trial to try Ksplice. The trial is available at https://www.ksplice.com/

After obtaining a key and creating an Uptrack account, the following steps will configure an Oracle Linux system to use Ksplice. The system must have access to the internet in order to install Ksplice. For systems that are using a proxy, set the proxy in the shell:

```
export http_proxy=http://proxy.company.com:port
export https_proxy=http://proxy.company.com:port
```

Execute the following commands as root, replacing ACCESS_KEY with the access key received upon sign-up:

```
wget -N https://www.ksplice.com/uptrack/install-uptrack
sh install-uptrack ACCESS_KEY
uptrack-upgrade -y
```

To configure Ksplice Uptrack to automatically install updates as they become available, the 'install-uptrack' command shown above can be run with the '--autoinstall' option:

```
sh install-uptrack YOUR_ACCESS_KEY --autoinstall
```

Alternately, you can set "autoinstall = yes" in the /etc/uptrack/uptrack.conf file after Ksplice has been installed

Manage Ksplice systems

The standard command to determine the kernel version of an Oracle Linux 6 system is the ‘uname –r’ command. In the example below, the kernel version is 2.6.39-200.24.1.el.

```
[root@matthew OL6_LOCAL]# uname -r
2.6.39-200.24.1.el6uek.x
```

However, for systems that have Ksplice uptrack service, it is recommended to use the 'uptrack-uname' command. The 'uptrack-uname' command accepts the same flags as the 'uname' command and displays the same effective output. Running the 'uptrack-uname –r' command to check the kernel version will generate the same output is same as 'uname –r' if the Ksplice uptrack service has not yet applied any kernel patches.

```
[root@matthew OL6_LOCAL]# uptrack-uname -r
2.6.39-200.24.1.el6uek.x
```

However, if the kernel has been updated using Ksplice and the system has not been rebooted since that time, then the 'uptrack-uname –r' and 'uname –r' commands will generate different results. 'uname –r' will show the version that was in place when Oracle Linux 6 was booted. The 'uptrack-uname –r' command will show the version number that the kernel has been patched to with Ksplice. Oracle does this by design because some applications may react badly if the kernel version changes underneath them while they are running. This is why it is recommended to use the 'uptrack-uname' command to get kernel information on Ksplice enabled systems.

There are several Uptrack service commands that are used to manage systems using Ksplice:

- **uptrack-upgrade** -- Install and apply an available Ksplice update.
- **uptrack-show** -- Display what Ksplice updates are installed on an Oracle Linux 6 system. When used with the '--available' option it will show any available updates on the Ksplice server.
- **uptrack-remove** -- Can remove all Ksplice updates by using the '--all' keyword or specific updates using the update IDs.

The main configuration file for the Ksplice uptrack service is the '/etc/uptrack/uptrack.conf' file. This is an ASCII file that can be viewed and edited with a standard text editor. You can use this file to configure your systems to automatically install updates as they become available by setting 'autoinstall = yes' in it.

Oracle Ksplice patches are stored locally on the file system in the '/var/cache/uptrack' directory. By default, these patches will automatically be re-applied after a reboot. The Ksplice repository configuration file is /etc/yum.repos.d/ksplice-uptrack.repo.

Automate tasks and System Logging

Describe available automated tasks utilities

Linux has three programs designed to execute tasks automatically. Each of the three serves different purposes:

- **cron** -- Cron is a daemon process that is used to execute commands at specific times of day, and/or specific days of the week or month. The daemon functions by waking up once every minute and consulting its configuration files to see if anything is scheduled to run in that minute. If there is a task to be run, it executes the required shell command and goes back to sleep for another minute. Cron is best suited for tasks that must be executed multiple times on a set schedule.
- **anacron** -- The cron utility is designed for Linux systems that run continuously. If a job is scheduled to run at noon on Saturday, but the system is not running at that time, cron will never run it even if the server were booted at 12:01. Anacron is designed to ensure that tasks that are scheduled to run on a daily, weekly, or monthly basis get run -- so long as the system is running at some portion during the appropriate interval. Unlike cron, anacron is not designed to ensure that tasks are executed at a specific time.
- **at** -- Where both cron and anacron are designed for tasks that are recurring, the at command is intended for scheduling one-off tasks that must occur at a future date. With the at command, you can schedule a given task to run at a precise supplied time in the future, or to run at a given offset from the current time (i.e. five hours from... now).

Configure cron jobs and use crontab utility

Running jobs at regular intervals is a task that is generally managed by the cron facility. The Linux cron capability consists of the crond daemon and a set of cron tables (also known as crontabs) that describe the work is to be done and how frequently. The crond daemon is usually started during the system startup by the init process. It wakes up once a minute to check the crontabs to see if anything needs to be started in the current minute.

Users manage the cron tables using the crontab command. The crontab command, like the passwd command, is an suid program that runs with root authority.

An example of a task that would be appropriate to schedule is backing up a file every night after work hours. The specific backup steps are irrelevant here, so for this example we will just say that the script **/var/script/backup.sh** will perform exactly the tasks we need if it is executed at the proper time. The intent is to execute the backup every weekday at 8PM.

In order to make the crond daemon execute the task automatically, we must use the crontab command to schedule the task. Running crontab with the -e option will open the cron table with the vi editor (unless you have specified a different editor with the EDITOR or VISUAL environment variables).

Every task to be executed in the crontab contains six fields:

- **Minute** -- Can range from 0-59
- **Hour** -- Can range from 0-23
- **Day of the month** -- Can range from 1-31
- **Month of the year** -- Can range from 1-12
- **Day of the week** -- Can be specified with 0-6 (with 0 being Sunday) or as sun, mon, tue, etc.
- **Task to execute** -- This is everything after the fifth field, and is interpreted as a string to pass to sh

Each of the time-related fields can specify an individual value, a range of values (such as 0-10 or sun-wed), or a comma-separated list of individual values and ranges (such as 1, 2, 5-7). An asterisk in a time field means there is no restriction based on the given time interval. Lines starting with a '#' symbol are comments.

When a task is executed by crond, a shell is opened and the commands executed from it. The environment of the cron shell is <u>not</u> that of the user's normal shell, so environment variables, paths, etc. will not be available by default. It is possible to add lines in the crontab to set up the shell environment that the tasks will execute in. A crontab entry to run the /var/script/backup.sh on every weekday at 8PM would look like the following:

```
# environment variables
SHELL=/bin/bash
PATH=/sbin:/bin:/usr/sbin:/usr/bin
00 20 * * 1-5 /var/script/backup.sh
```

In this example, reading the parameters in order, the command is executed at the 0th minute for the 20th hour no matter what day of the month it is or what month of the year it is every weekday (Monday-Friday). The weekdays could also have been specified as 'mon-fri', or '1,2,3,4,5' or 'mon,tue,wed,thu,fri':

```
00 20 * * mon-fri /var/script/backup.sh
00 20 * * 1,2,3,4,5 /var/script/backup.sh
00 20 * * mon,tue,wed,thu,fri /var/script/backup.sh
```

The files created with the crontab command are stored in /etc/spool/cron under the name of the user who created it. In addition to these user crontab files, crond also checks /etc/crontab and files in the /etc/cron.d directory. These contain system crontab files. System crontabs have one additional field between the fifth time entry (day) and the command. The additional field specifies the user for whom the command should be run (normally this is root).

Configure anacron jobs

The anacron facility (for "anachronistic cron") is designed to handle scheduling of daily, weekly, or monthly jobs just as the cron facility does. However, cron jobs are scheduled for a specific time and will only be executed if the system is running at the time they are scheduled for. Anacron cannot be configured to handle hourly jobs.

Unlike cron jobs, anacron jobs are not scheduled to run at a specific time. Instead they are configured with a specific frequency. Anacron maintains timestamp files in the /var/spool/anacron directory that record when jobs are executed. When anacron runs, it will check the timestamp files to see if the required number of days has passed since a given job was last run. If the specified interval has elapsed, the job is executed. The table of jobs for anacron is stored in /etc/anacrontab. Anacrontab files have a markedly different format than crontab files. Each job has four fields:

- **period** -- Can be specified as a number of days or as @daily, @weekly, @monthly, or @yearly. This will ensure jobs are run once a week, month or year no matter the number of days in the period.
- **delay** -- The number of minutes to wait after the system is started before executing any jobs that are due to run.
- **job-identifier** -- The job-identifier can contain any non-blank character, except slashes. It is used to identify the job in anacron messages, and as the name for the job's timestamp file.
- **command** -- This is the command to be executed.

Comments and environment lines can be placed in an anacron file just as with a crontab file. There are two variables used by anacron in determining when to run jobs.

- **START_HOURS_RANGE** -- determines the portion of the day in which anacron will execute jobs.

- **RANDOM_DELAY** -- This variable will add a random number of minutes (up to the specified value) to the start time of a job. This helps to spread jobs out if several are ready to run at startup, or alternately if several are ready to run at the beginning of the window specified by the START_HOURS_RANGE variable.

The following is a reasonably close equivalent of the crontab file created earlier. Anacron will try to run the /var/script/backup.sh daily between the hours of eight and 10 P.M.

```
# environment variables
SHELL=/bin/sh
PATH=/sbin:/bin:/usr/sbin:/usr/bin
# Anacron jobs will start between 8pm and 10pm
START_HOURS_RANGE=20-22
RANDOM_DELAY=45
1        0    backup.daily          /var/script/backup.sh
```

Observe contents of rsyslog configuration file

Rsyslogd is an open source software utility designed to provide support for message logging. The logging is provided by rsyslogd, an enhanced, multi-threaded syslog daemon which replaces sysklogd. It provides the same functionality as syslogd and extends it with enhanced filtering, encryption protected relaying of messages, and support for transportation via the TCP or UDP protocols. Rsyslog supports MySQL, PostgreSQL, failover log destinations, syslog/tcp, fine grain output format control, high precision timestamps, queued operations and the ability to filter on any message part. It has a close compatibility with the older syslogd utility and can often be used as a drop-in replacement. It is easy to configure, but has the capability to provide enterprise-class, encryption protected syslog relay chains. Every message logged by rsyslogd contains at least a time and a hostname field, and normally a program name field. It supports free definition of output formats via templates. Rsyslog supports precise timestamps and can write directly to a database.

The rsyslog logging utility is configured via the rsyslog.conf file, typically found in /etc. By default, rsyslogd reads the file /etc/rsyslog.conf. This may be changed by starting rsyslogd using the command line option "-f".

Efforts have been made to keep the configuration file as compatible as possible with the older syslog utility. Rsyslogd will normally work with a standard syslog.conf file. That said, to use many of the enhanced features of rqyslog will require a different config file syntax. A snippet of an rsyslog.conf file is shown below:

```
# rsyslog v5 configuration file

# For more information see /usr/share/doc/rsyslog-*/rsyslog_conf.html
# If you experience problems, see http://www.rsyslog.com/doc/troubleshoot.html

#### MODULES ####

$ModLoad imuxsock # provides support for local system logging (e.g. via logger comman
d)
$ModLoad imklog   # provides kernel logging support (previously done by rklogd)
#$ModLoad immark  # provides --MARK-- message capability

# Provides UDP syslog reception
#$ModLoad imudp
#$UDPServerRun 514

# Provides TCP syslog reception
#$ModLoad imtcp
#$InputTCPServerRun 514


#### GLOBAL DIRECTIVES ####

# Use default timestamp format
$ActionFileDefaultTemplate RSYSLOG_TraditionalFileFormat

# File syncing capability is disabled by default. This feature is usually not require
d,
# not useful and an extreme performance hit
#$ActionFileEnableSync on
```

Rsyslogd has several different classes of loadable modules:

- **Input Modules** -- These are used to gather messages from various sources. They interface to message generators.
- **Output Modules** -- These process messages. With them, message formats can be transformed and messages be transmitted to various different targets.
- **Parser Modules** -- These are used to parse message content, once the message has been received. They can be used to process custom message formats or invalidly formatted messages.
- **Message Modification Modules** -- These are used to change the content of messages being processed. They can be implemented using either the output module or the parser module interface.
- **String Generator Modules** -- Used to generate strings based on the message content.

- **Library Modules** -- Provide dynamically loadable functionality for parts of rsyslog, most often for other loadable modules.

Describe rsyslog actions and templates

Actions specify what rsyslog is to do with the messages filtered out by a given selector. Some of the actions that can be defined include:

- **Syslog message placement** -- Most actions specify which log file a message should be saved to. The specified file path can be either static or dynamic.
- **Sending syslog messages over the network** -- Rsyslog has the ability to send and receive messagee over the network. Using this feature, rsyslog can administer syslog messages of multiple hosts on a single machine.
- **Sending syslog messages to specific users** -- It is posisble to send send syslog messages to specific users by specifying the username(s) to send the messages to. To specify more than one user, separate each username with a comma (,). To send messages to every user that is currently logged on, use an asterisk (*).
- **Discarding syslog messages** -- It is possible to discard messages that do not need to be logged. The tilde character (~) is ued to discard selected messages.

Templates are used to format every output generated by rsyslog. This includes files, user messages, messages written to log files, etc. The format of a template is dependent on the type of output being generated. When using the database writer to log messages to a database, for example, the template would be a SQL statement. Templates compatible with the stock syslogd formats are hardcoded into rsyslogd. These are used when no template is specified.

Configure rsyslog to log debug messages

Global directives specify configuration options that apply to the rsyslogd daemon. They usually specify a value for a specific pre-defined variable that affects the behavior of the rsyslogd daemon or a rule that follows. Only one global directive may be specified per line and they always start with a dollar sign ($). For example, the default maximum size of the syslog message queue is 10,000 messages. This value can be overridden by specifying a different value using a global directive as follows:

```
$MainMsgQueueSize 40000
```

Multiple directives can be defined in in the /etc/rsyslog.conf configuration file. A given directive will affect the behavior of all configuration options until a second occurrence of that same directive occurs.

A rule in rsyslog is specified by a filter part and an action part. The filter selects a subset of syslog messages. The action specifies what to do with the selected messages. To create a rule in the '/etc/rsyslog.conf' configuration file, define a filter and an action on a single line separated by one or more spaces or tabs.

Messages are filtered based on two conditions: facility and priority.

- **Facility** -- This can be represented by one of the following keywords: auth, authpriv, cron, daemon, kern, lpr, mail, news, syslog, user, uucp, and local0 through local7.
- **Priority** -- This specifies the priority of a syslog message. It can be represented by any of the following keywords: debug, info, notice, warning, err, crit, alert, and emerg.

The syntax for a filter is Facility.Priority. An example of a filter that would log all critical and higher priority messages for the mail rsyslog facility would be:

```
mail.crit
```

A portion of the rules section of the /etc/rsyslog.conf file is below:

```
#### RULES ####

# Log all kernel messages to the console.
# Logging much else clutters up the screen.
#kern.*                                                 /dev/console

# Log anything (except mail) of level info or higher.
# Don't log private authentication messages!
*.info;mail.none;authpriv.none;cron.none                /var/log/messages

# The authpriv file has restricted access.
authpriv.*                                              /var/log/secure

# Log all the mail messages in one place.
mail.*                                                 -/var/log/maillog

# Log cron stuff
cron.*                                                  /var/log/cron
```

In the section of the /etc/rsyslog.conf file shown above, you can you see that all messages of level 'info' and higher will be logged in the /var/log/messages file. However, rsyslogd will not log mail messages, private authentication messages, or cron messages there.

The available priority levels from lowest to highest are:

- **debug** -- Debug-level messages
- **info** -- Informational messages
- **notice** -- Normal bug significant condition
- **warning** -- Warning conditions
- **err** -- Error conditions
- **crit** -- Critical conditions
- **alert** -- Action must be taken immediately
- **emerg** -- System is unstable

Because debug message are lower than info messages, the *.info rule will not log any debug messages (but it will log notice, warning, err, crit, alert, and emerg messages). To make rsyslogd log debug messages, edit the /etc/rsyslog.conf file and change the line to read:

```
*.debug;mail.none;authpriv.none;cron.none        /var/log/messages
```

After changing the rule and saving the file, the rsyslogd daemon must be restarted. The daemon only reads the /etc/rsyslog.conf when it starts up. Once restarted, messages of debug level and higher (i.e. all messages minus the three exceptions noted above) will be logged to the /var/log/messages file.

```
[root@matthew etc]# service rsyslog restart
Shutting down system logger:                               [  OK  ]
Starting system logger:                                    [  OK  ]
```

It is also possible to log a range of messages. The directive below tells rsyslogd to save all kernel messages that come with priorities from info up to warning in the file /var/adm/kernel-info. Everything from err and higher is excluded.

```
kern.info;kern.!err /var/adm/kernel-info
```

Some of the common log files are:

- **anaconda.log** -- Logs and messages from Linux Anaconda installer
- **audit** -- Directory for audit events/information logged by auditd daemon
- **boot.log** -- Contains information logged when system boots
- **cron** -- Cron jobs information logged by crond daemon
- **dmesg** -- Contains kernel ring buffer log information which is information about the hardware devices that the kernel detects during boot process.
- **httpd** -- Directory contains apache web server access and error logs
- **messages** -- File contains global system messages. Includes messages that are logged during system startup.
- **yum.log** -- Yum command log information about package management tasks like install, update, erase etc.

User and Group Administration

Create users and groups using command-line utilities

When users and groups are created on a Linux system, there are several files that influence the behavior of the account creation process. You should understand the impact of these files before creating users or groups. The first of the files is /etc/default/useradd. This file sets several defaults for new accounts. An example is shown below:

```
# useradd defaults file
GROUP=100
HOME=/home
INACTIVE=-1
EXPIRE=
SHELL=/bin/bash
SKEL=/etc/skel
CREATE_MAIL_SPOOL=yes
```

Alternately, you can run the useradd with the -D option to see the default values:

```
[root@matthew etc]# useradd -D
GROUP=100
HOME=/home
INACTIVE=-1
EXPIRE=
SHELL=/bin/bash
SKEL=/etc/skel
CREATE_MAIL_SPOOL=yes
```

The variables in the file and their meanings are:

- **GROUP** -- The group name or number of the user's initial login group.
- **HOME** -- The default base for user home directories.
- **INACTIVE** -- The number of days after a password expires until the account is permanently disabled. A value of 0 disables the account as soon as the password has expired, and a value of -1 disables the feature.

- **EXPIRE** -- The default expiration data for the account.
- **SHELL** -- The default user shell.
- **SKEL** -- The skeleton directory, which contains files and directories to be copied in the user's home directory.
- **CREATE_MAIL_SPOOL** -- Determines whether or not to create a users mail spool file in /var/spool/mail/.

The contents of the directory specified by the 'SKEL' variable are copied to a user's home directory when the user is created. If there is a file that you would like all new users to receive, such as instructions for new users or a welcome packet, then you can add a file to that directory. Every user created after that file is added will receive a copy (but not user accounts that already exist).

```
[root@matthew etc]# ls -al /etc/skel
total 44
drwxr-xr-x. 4 root root  4096 Sep 21 22:50 .
drwxr-xr-x. 113 root root 12288 Sep 19 18:00 ..
-rw-r--r--. 1 root root    18 May 10  2012 .bash_logout
-rw-r--r--. 1 root root   176 May 10  2012 .bash_profile
-rw-r--r--. 1 root root   124 May 10  2012 .bashrc
drwxr-xr-x. 2 root root  4096 Nov 20  2010 .gnome2
-rw-r--r--. 1 root root   121 Jul  8 06:59 .kshrc
drwxr-xr-x. 4 root root  4096 Sep 10 13:54 .mozilla
-rw-r--r--. 1 root root   658 Apr 29  2012 .zshrc
```

Another file that is central to the creation of new user accounts is /etc/login.defs. This file defines the configuration for the shadow password suite. It is a text file that defines a number of parameters associated with shadow passwords. It also defines several aspects related to user accounts such as password aging and encryption method, the permission mask, user and group ID minimum and maximum values, etc.

```
# Please note that the parameters in this configuration file control the
# behavior of the tools from the shadow-utils component. None of these
# tools uses the PAM mechanism, and the utilities that use PAM (such as the
# passwd command) should therefore be configured elsewhere. Refer to
# /etc/pam.d/system-auth for more information.
#

# *REQUIRED*
#   Directory where mailboxes reside, _or_ name of file, relative to the
#   home directory.  If you _do_ define both, MAIL_DIR takes precedence.
#   QMAIL_DIR is for Qmail
#
#QMAIL_DIR      Maildir
MAIL_DIR        /var/spool/mail
#MAIL_FILE      .mail

# Password aging controls:
#
#       PASS_MAX_DAYS   Maximum number of days a password may be used.
#       PASS_MIN_DAYS   Minimum number of days allowed between password changes.
#       PASS_MIN_LEN    Minimum acceptable password length.
#       PASS_WARN_AGE   Number of days warning given before a password expires.
#
PASS_MAX_DAYS   99999
PASS_MIN_DAYS   0
PASS_MIN_LEN    5
PASS_WARN_AGE   7
```

Some of the command line utilities that are involved in user and group administration include:

- **useradd** -- Add user accounts
- **usermod** -- Modify user accounts
- **userdel** -- Delete user accounts
- **users** -- Print the user names of users logged in on the host
- **groupadd** -- Add groups
- **groupmod** -- Modify groups
- **groupdel** -- Delete groups
- **groups** -- Print the groups a user is in
- **gpasswd** -- Administer /etc/gshadow and /etc/group files

The example below creates a new user account for the user Tim Ployee:

```
[root@matthew etc]# useradd -c "Tim Ployee" tployee
```

Since Tim is a contract employee, the following command will add a new 'contractors' group. Then tployee will be added to the group and the groups command will be used to verify the change.

```
[root@matthew etc]# groupadd contractors
[root@matthew etc]# usermod -G contractors tployee
[root@matthew etc]# groups tployee
tployee : tployee contractors
```

Use the id command to verify user information and manually review passwd and group files

The id command is used to display user and group information for a specified username. When no username is supplied, it will display information for the current user. Running the command for the tployee user created in the previous section returns the following:

```
[root@matthew etc]# id tployee
uid=54324(tployee) gid=54325(tployee)
groups=54325(tployee),54326(contractors)
```

From left to right, the information shown is user id and name, effective group id and name, and a comma-separated list of all groups and names of which tployee is a member. This confirms that the steps taken in the previous section worked as advertised.

The options of the id command are used to limit the information returned by the command. For example, using the –g flag will return only the effective group ID of the user. The –gn option will return only the name of the effective group that the user belongs to, and the –G option prints all the group IDs of a user.

```
[root@matthew etc]# id -g tployee
54325
[root@matthew etc]# id -gn tployee
tployee
[root@matthew etc]# id -G tployee
54325 54326
```

Another method for viewing (or verifying) information about a user account is to look in one of three files in the /etc directory.

- **/etc/passwd** -- This is a text-based database of information about users that may log in to the system or other operating system user identities that own running processes.
- **/etc/shadow** -- This file increases the security level of passwords by storing hashed password data separate from the /etc/passwd file and restricting access to all but privileged users.
- **/etc/group** -- This file defines the groups to which users belong.

```
[root@matthew etc]# cat /etc/passwd | grep tployee
tployee:x:54324:54325:Tim Ployee:/home/tployee:/bin/bash
```

The fields in all three files are delimited by colons. The fields in the /etc/passwd are, from left to right:

- Username
- Encrypted password (or 'x' if shadow passwords are in effect)
- User ID
- Default group ID
- Full name
- Home directory
- Default shell

```
[root@matthew etc]# cat /etc/shadow | grep tployee
tployee:!!:15970:0:99999:7:::
```

The fields in /etc/shadow are, from left to right:

- Userid
- Encrypted password,
- Days since Jan 1, 1970 that password was last changed
- Days before password may be changed
- Days after which password must be changed
- Days before password is to expire that user is warned

- Days after password expires that account is disabled
- Days since Jan 1, 1970 that account is disabled
- A reserved field

```
[root@matthew etc]# cat /etc/group | grep tployee
tployee:x:54325:
contractors:x:54326:tployee
```

The fields in the /etc/group file are, from left to right:

- Group name
- Encrypted group password (or x if shadow passwords are in use)
- Group ID
- Group members' usernames, comma-separated

When Tim's contract expires, the userdel command can be user to remove his account. Once that has been done, checking the three files shows no sign that he ever existed:

```
[root@matthew etc]# userdel tployee
[root@matthew etc]# cat /etc/passwd | grep tployee
[root@matthew etc]# cat /etc/shadow | grep tployee
[root@matthew etc]# cat /etc/group | grep tployee
```

Configure password aging

Password aging is a technique used by system administrators to attempt to increase system security. The thought is that changing password over time will help reduce the chance of having compromised passwords. The reality is that users will generally use a rotating set of bad passwords (i.e. badpass1, badpass2, badpass3, badpass4...). This is not likely to be a test question... just the author being cynical.

When password aging is enabled, after a set amount of time the user is prompted to select a new password. Oracle Linux 6 has two ways in which it is possible to specify password aging. Aging can be configured using the chage command-line utility or it can be done from the User Manager Tool.

The User Manager tool was discussed earlier. Password aging can be configured from the 'Password Info' tab of the User Properties control.

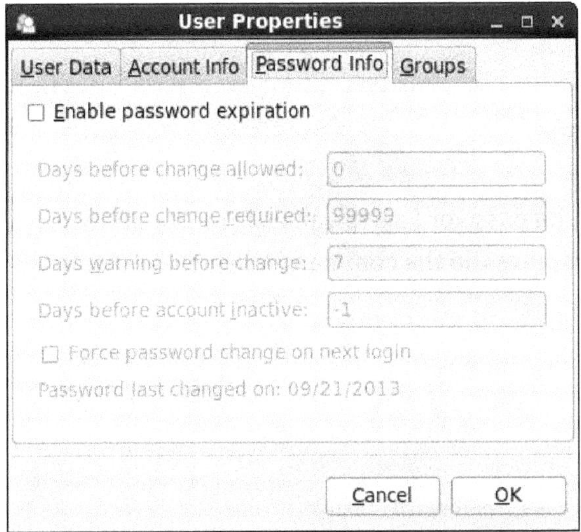

The chage utility can perform all of the same password aging functions as the User Manager Tool. Typing chage at the command prompt with no parameters will provide the usage screen:

```
[root@matthew etc]# chage
Usage: chage [options] [LOGIN]

Options:
  -d, --lastday LAST_DAY        set date of last password change to LAST_DAY
  -E, --expiredate EXPIRE_DATE  set account expiration date to EXPIRE_DATE
  -h, --help                    display this help message and exit
  -I, --inactive INACTIVE       set password inactive after expiration
                                to INACTIVE
  -l, --list                    show account aging information
  -m, --mindays MIN_DAYS        set minimum number of days before password
                                change to MIN_DAYS
  -M, --maxdays MAX_DAYS        set maximim number of days before password
                                change to MAX_DAYS
  -W, --warndays WARN_DAYS      set expiration warning days to WARN_DAYS
```

The previous section noted that many of the fields in the /etc/shadow file are for password aging information. Since Tim's contract has ended, the below example looks at the data for inewuser:

```
[root@matthew etc]# cat /etc/shadow | grep inewuser
inewuser:$6$irsgjn2hUclABZbe$rQQuKy3xDLiET2Uf1.f0wEK7ES1ODQMRKYp01Xpv
v4F9sE.py340fhpZ3hnZyMMa559auBqrsMgcWXfn/B9T8/:15969:0:99999:7:::
```

It is possible to determine the password aging values from the above. However, it is much easier to use the the command 'chage -l' to display them:

```
[root@matthew etc]# chage -l inewuser
Last password change                                    : Sep 21, 2013
Password expires                                        : never
Password inactive                                       : never
Account expires                                         : never
Minimum number of days between password change          : 0
Maximum number of days between password change          : 99999
Number of days of warning before password expires       : 7
```

The following example will change the password aging for inewuser to have a minimum password age of 15 days, a maximum of 90 days, and allow a 7 day warning period that the password will be expiring:

```
[root@matthew etc]# chage inewuser
Changing the aging information for inewuser
Enter the new value, or press ENTER for the default

    Minimum Password Age [0]: 15
    Maximum Password Age [99999]: 90
    Last Password Change (YYYY-MM-DD) [2013-09-21]:
    Password Expiration Warning [7]:
    Password Inactive [-1]:
    Account Expiration Date (YYYY-MM-DD) [1969-12-31
```

After performing the update, the 'chage -l' command can be used to verify that the password aging values have been altered:

```
[root@matthew etc]# chage -l inewuser
Last password change                                    : Sep 21, 2013
Password expires                                        : Dec 20, 2013
Password inactive                                       : never
Account expires                                         : never
Minimum number of days between password change          : 15
Maximum number of days between password change          : 90
Number of days of warning before password expires       : 7
```

The values in the /etc/shadow file password aging related fields have also been modified.

```
[root@matthew etc]# cat /etc/shadow | grep inewuser
inewuser:$6$irsgjn2hUclABZbe$rQQuKy3xDLiET2Uf1.f0wEK7ES1ODQMRKYp01Xpv
v4F9sE.py340fhpZ3hnZyMMa559auBqrsMgcWXfn/B9T8/:15969:15:90:7:
```

Use the User Manager GUI tool

The User Manager GUI tool allows you to view, modify, add, and delete local users and groups. The tool can be started from the Desktop by selecting the System-> Administration-> Users and Groups option from the Desktop menu panel. It is also possible to start the tool from the command line by executing the command 'system-configusers'. Regardless of which method is used to start it, if you run the application as a regular Linux user, the application will prompt you to authenticate as root. Once launched, you will see the following GUI window (with a different set of user accounts):

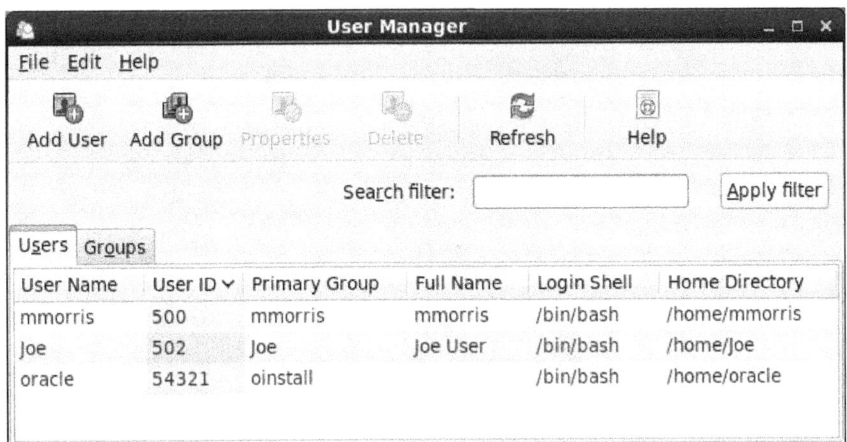

The Users and Groups displayed in the User Manager Application do not include the system users and groups by default. This can be changed by unchecking the 'Hide system users and groups' option in the Edit->Preferences screen. Click the 'Add User' button in the User Manager Tool to create a new user. Fill in the username, full name and password and confirm password fields. Optionally you can select a login shell and home directory that is different from the default.

Oracle Linux 6 uses a User Private Group (UPG) scheme by default. A UPG is created whenever a new user is added to the system. It has the same name as the user for which it was created and that user is the only member of the group. UPGs make it safe to set default permissions for a newly created file or directory, allowing both the user and the group of that user to make modifications to the file or directory. It is also possible to specify the Group ID (GID) and User ID (UID) manually by entering a value. By default Oracle Linux and RHEL reserve UIDs and GIDs below 500 for system users and groups.

After a new user has been created, the account will be listed under the 'Users' tab of the application window. Selecting the user and clicking the 'Properties' option will bring up the properties screen. From this window, it is possible to change the details entered in the original account creation, lock the account or set it to expire, set password restrictions, and view or change what groups the user is in.

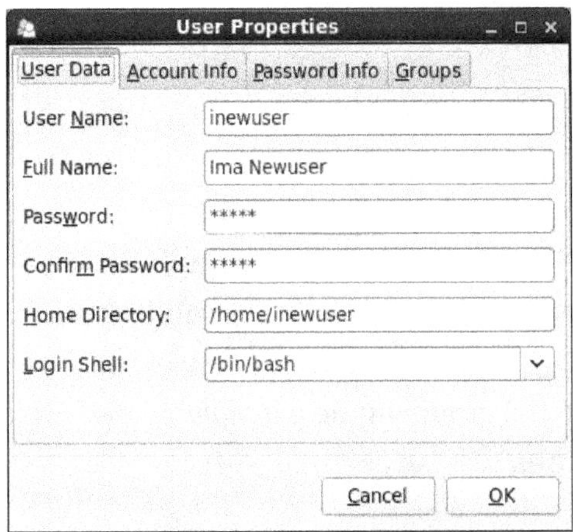

The User Manager Tool can also be used for groups administration. Groups are administered by clicking on the 'Groups' tab of the User Manager Tool. The initial screen shows all of the groups available on the system.

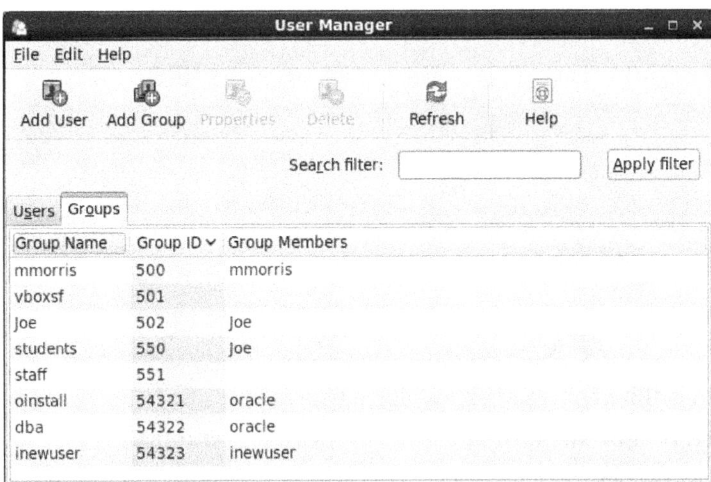

To add a new group, click the 'Add Group' menu item. The only mandatory field to enter is a group name. You can optionally select a group number.

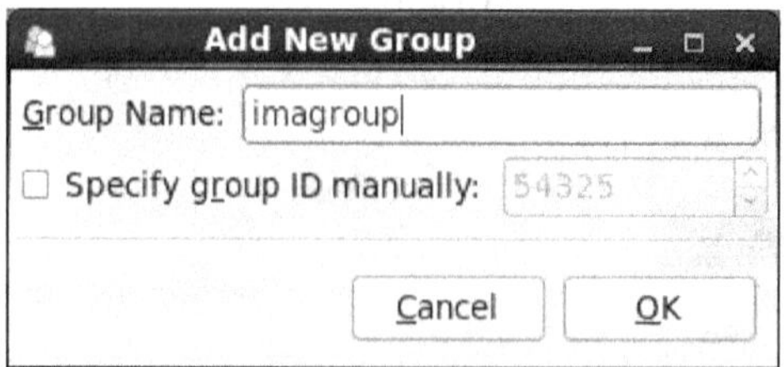

Selecting a group and clicking the 'Properties' menu item brings up the group properties screen. This screen has considerably fewer options than that of users. It allows you to change the group name and to view or change which users are assigned to the group. In the example below, inewuser has been added to the group.

Describe LDAP and NIS authentication options

Authentication is the mechanism by which a user is identified and verified on a system. As part of the authentication process, a user must supply their identity and some form of credentials. The most common form of authentication is for users to supply a username and password. However, smart card authentication is also common. Authentication with a smart card requires that you physically insert the card into a reader and then enter a Personal Identification Number (PIN). Biometric authentication that uses fingerprint or retinal scans is becoming more common as the technology for this improves and the cost of implementation decreases. Systems that must be extremely secure might combine two or more of these authentication methods.

The default authentication for Oracle Linux 6, and the only one discussed so far relies on local password files (/etc/passwd or /etc/shadow) when authenticating users to the system. The LDAP and NIS authentication methods use remote authentication. The data used to authenticate users is stored on a different server than the one they are connecting to.

NIS

The Network Information Service (NIS) is a client–server directory service protocol for distributing system configuration data such as user and host names between computers on a computer network. Originally called Yellow pages or YP, it was developed by Sun Microsystems, but has since been licensed to virtually all other Unix vendors. An NIS system maintains a central directory of user and group information, hostnames, e-mail aliases and other information. The information is distributed to the NIS clients that use it for authentication. Any number of Linux systems can be configured to make use of the information in the central NIS server for authentication.

LDAP:

The Lightweight Directory Access Protocol is a standard technology for network directories. Network directories are specialized databases that contain information about people, devices, applications and other aspects of a computer network. The protocol is based on a client-server model. LDAP servers provide the directory service, and LDAP clients use the directory service to access entries and attributes. A client will start an

LDAP session by connecting to an LDAP server that listens on TCP port 389 (by default). A request is sent from the client to the server, which will then respond with the information required.

The Authentication Configuration tool is used to select the authentication databases and configure the associated options. It has both GUI and command-line options to configure any user data stores. The GUI can be launched by using executing 'system-config-authentication' from the command line. Alternately you can launch it by clicking the System -> Administration -> Authentication menu option.

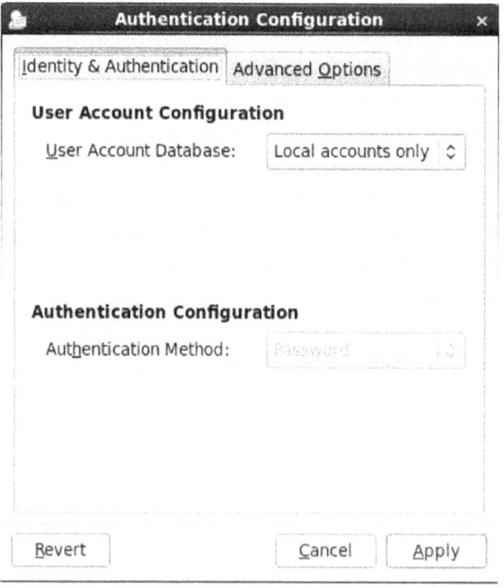

The Authentication Configuration Tool contains two tabs:

- **Identity & Authentication** -- The controls in this tab provide the ability to configure the resource used as the identity store. The User Accounts Database control defines how users should be authenticated. The Authentication configuration control allows you to select methods appropriate to the databases uses. For example, when LDAP is selected, you can choose between using Kerberos and LDAP passwords.

- **Advanced Options** -- This tab allows for the selection of authentication methods other than passwords or certificates, such as fingerprint readers or smart cards. It also allows local access control to be enabled.

The available user account databases are:

- **Local accounts only** -- Local /etc/passwd and /etc/shadow files
- **LDAP** -– LDAP server and base DN configuration
- **IPAv2** –- IPA Domain, server, realm configuration
- **NIS** -- NIS Server and domain configuration
- **Winbind** -- Winbind authentication

Perform basic Pluggable Authentication Modules (PAM) configuration and configure LDAP authentication

Pluggable Authentication Modules (PAM) provide a common framework for authentication and security. Many programs are configured to use PAM as a centralized authentication mechanism. The modular architecture affords the system administrator considerable flexibility in setting authentication policies. PAM is a useful system for both developers and administrators for several reasons:

- Provides a common authentication scheme that can be used with a wide variety of applications.
- Offers significant flexibility and control over authentication.
- There is single, fully-documented library which allows developers to write programs without having to write authentication schemes from ground zero.

The PAM authentication mechanism allows you to configure how applications can use authentication to verify the identity of users. The configuration files are in the /etc/pam.d directory. Every PAM-aware application has a file in this directory. The file will usually have the same name as the service to which it controls access. Every PAM-aware application must define its service name and install its own PAM configuration file. For example, the login program defines its service name as login and installs the /etc/pam.d/login PAM configuration file.

PAM configuration file contain directives that define the module and any controls or arguments with it. The directives are:

- **module_interface** –- Four types of PAM module interface are available: auth, account, password, session
- **control_flag** –- All PAM modules generate a success or failure result when called. Control flags tell PAM what do with the result. The possible flags are: required, requisite, sufficient, optional, include
- **module_name** -– The module name provides PAM with the name of the pluggable module containing the specified module interface.
- **module_arguments** -– PAM uses arguments to pass information to a pluggable module during authentication for some modules.

For example, in the following line, the module_interface is 'auth', the control_flag is 'required' and the module name is 'pam_securetty.so'. There are no arguments.

```
auth       required  pam_securetty.so
```

Below is the /etc/pam.d/reboot PAM configuration file. Each line starts with the module_interface name, next is the control_flag, third field is the module name and the fourth field (if it exists) is the arguments for the module.

```
[root@matthew pam.d]# cat reboot
#%PAM-1.0
auth        sufficient  pam_rootok.so
auth        required    pam_console.so
#auth        include    system-auth
account     required    pam_permit.s
```

In the above example, the lines are processed as follows (minus the first line which is a comment):

- **auth sufficient pam_rootok.so** — This line uses the pam_rootok.so module to check whether the current user is root, by verifying that their UID is 0. If this test succeeds, no other modules are consulted and the command is executed. If this test fails, the next module is consulted.
- **auth required pam_console.so** — This line uses the pam_console.so module to attempt to authenticate the user. If this user is already logged in at the console, pam_console.so checks whether there is a file in the /etc/security/console.apps/ directory with the same name as the service name (reboot). If such a file exists, authentication succeeds and control is passed to the next module.
- **#auth include system-auth** — This line is commented and is not processed.
- **account required pam_permit.so** — This line uses the pam_permit.so module to allow the root user or anyone logged in at the console to reboot the system.

LDAP can be configured either from the Authentication Configuration Tool GUI or from the command line. If using the GUI, launch the application tool and select LDAP as the user account database. You must supply the LDAP Search Base DN and the LDAP Server that will be used. The LDAP authentication method can use either LDAP or Kerberos passwords.

It is also possible to configure LDAP from the command line. The authconfig command-line utility will update all of the configuration files and services required for system authentication. You can use the --enableldap option to use an LDAP identity store. In order to use LDAP as the authentication source, you can use the '--enableldapauth' option of authconfig. You must then provide additional information such as the LDAP server name, base DN for the user suffix, and so on. Whenever using authconfig, you must include either the --update or --test option. One of those options is required for the command to run successfully. Using --update writes the configuration changes. --test prints the changes to stdout but does not apply the changes to the configuration. An example authcofig command is shown below:

```
authconfig --enableldap --enableldapauth --
ldapserver=ldap://ldap.example.com:389 --
ldapbasedn="ou=people,dc=example,dc=com" --enableldaptls --
ldaploadcacert=https://ca.server.example.com/caCert.crt --update
```

Oracle Linux File Systems and Storage Administration

Describe disk partitioning and disk partitioning utilities

Disk partitioning is the act of dividing a hard disk drive into multiple logical storage units. Each storage unit is referred to as a partition and allows the operating system to treat one physical disk drive as if it were multiple disks. Because the partitions are treated separately, different file systems can be used on each partition. Software programs known as partition editors are used to create, resize, delete, and manipulate partitions on the hard drive. A given partition will consist of a range of cylinders on the physical drive. The size of cylinders is variable based on the hardware.

There are several disk partitioning tools available in Linux. This chapter will describe three of the more common utilities: fdisk, parted, and cfdisk. Partitioning editors are run while connected to the server as the root user. Partitioning is an inherently destructive operation that is not available to normal users.

fdisk

The fdisk utility is one of the most commonly used partition editors. It allows you to view, edit, and delete disk partitions. The below example shows the result of running the fdisk command with the -l option to list the partition tables for the specified devices. It provides the size of the drive, the number of cylinders, partition information for the drive, and more.

```
[root@matthew pam.d]# fdisk -l

Disk /dev/sda: 12.9 GB, 12884901888 bytes
255 heads, 63 sectors/track, 1566 cylinders
Units = cylinders of 16065 * 512 = 8225280 bytes
```

```
Sector size (logical/physical): 512 bytes / 512 bytes
I/O size (minimum/optimal): 512 bytes / 512 bytes
Disk identifier: 0x000654ad

   Device Boot      Start         End      Blocks   Id  System
/dev/sda1   *           1          64      512000   83  Linux
Partition 1 does not end on cylinder boundary.
/dev/sda2              64        1567    12069888   8e  Linux LVM
```

parted

The parted GNU utility is another editor that is commonly used to manipulate partition table of Linux systems. While not as commonly used as fdisk, it has advantages over it when working with drives over two terabytes in size. The parted also has a -l option that will list drive and partition information. Below is a snippet of the results from that command:

```
[root@matthew pam.d]# parted -l
Model: ATA VBOX HARDDISK (scsi)
Disk /dev/sda: 12.9GB
Sector size (logical/physical): 512B/512B
Partition Table: msdos

Number  Start   End     Size    Type     File system  Flags
 1      1049kB  525MB   524MB   primary  ext4         boot
 2      525MB   12.9GB  12.4GB  primary               lvm
```

cfdisk

The cfdisk utility is another disk partitioning tool that is available on Linux. As with fdisk and parted, it can be used to view, modify and delete partition tables. The -Ps option of the cfdisk utility can be used to display partition information.

```
[root@matthew pam.d]# cfdisk -Ps
Partition Table for /dev/sda

             First      Last
# Type       Sector    Sector    Offset  Length    Filesystem Type Flag
- -------- ------- ---------- ------ --------- --------------- ----
  Pri/Log        0      2047*     0#      2048*Free Space      None
1 Primary     2048*  1026047*     0    1024000*Linux (83)      Boot
2 Primary  1026048* 25165823*     0   24139776*Linux LVM (8E)  None
```

Describe supported file system types (ext2, ext3, ext4, Vfat, btrfs,ocfs2,nfs)

A filesystem determines how the storage of data (i.e., files, folders, etc.) is organized on a computer disk. This is the case no matter what the disk actually is. It may be a hard disk, floppy disk, CDROM/DVD, USB thumb drive, a partition on a hard disk, or a virtual drive created by virtualization software. There are a number of file systems available for Linux. Each has its own set of rules for controlling the allocation of disk space to files and for associating data about each file. Data about the files is referred to as meta data and includes information such as its filename, the directory in which it is located, its permissions and its creation date.

ext2

The ext2 (second extended filesystem) was designed as a replacement for the extended file system (ext). ext2 was the default filesystem in several Linux distributions, including Red Hat Linux, until it was replaced by ext3. The ext2 filesystem is still the preferred choice for flash-based storage media because it does not perform journaling. This increases performance and minimizes the number of writes. Since flash devices have a limited number of write cycles, ext2 extends their lifespan.

ext3

ext3 (third extended filesystem), is a journaled file system that is the default file system for many popular Linux distributions. Its main advantage over ext2 is journaling. This improves reliability and eliminates the need to check the file system after an unclean shutdown. The ext3 filesystem does not perform as well as competing Linux filesystems, such as ext4, JFS, ReiserFS and XFS. However, it allows in-place upgrades from ext2 without having to back up and restore data. It is also considered safer than many other Linux file systems, due to its relative simplicity and broad usage.

ext4

ext4 (fourth extended filesystem), can support volumes with sizes up to 1 exbibyte (EiB) and files with sizes up to 16 tebibytes (TiB). ext4 replaced the block mapping scheme used by ext2 and ext3 with extents. An extent is a range of contiguous physical blocks. Using extents in lieu of block mapping improves large file performance and reduces fragmentation. ext4 is backward compatible with ext3 and ext2, making it possible to mount ext3 and ext2 filesystems as ext4.

vfat

Vfat is a variant of the FAT (File Allocation Table) filesystem. The original FAT filesystem had an 8.3 filename structure. Filenames could have a maximum of eleven characters – eight, then a period, then a three-character extension. The vfat filesystem driver provides long filename support using the same disk data structures that Microsoft Windows uses for VFAT long filename support on FAT format volumes. However, the VFAT filesystem does not support any extra Linux file semantics. Because its data structures are the same as those used by Windows for VFAT long filenames, if Windows and Linux machines both access the drive, the data structures will not become unsynchronized. For this reason, VFAT is generally the most appropriate filesystem driver to use when sharing data on a FAT disk volume between Linux and Windows operating systems.

btrfs

Btrfs is a GPL-licensed experimental copy-on-write file system for Linux. The filesystem is still in development and marked as unstable. Btrfs is intended to address the lack of pooling, snapshots, checksums, and integral multi-device spanning in Linux file systems. These features will become crucial as Linux use scales upward into the larger storage configurations common in enterprise systems. Btrfs can have up to a 16 Exabyte volume size with billions of sub volumes. It has built-in RAID, transparent data integrity, and is optimized for solid-state devices.

ocfs2

OCFS2 (Oracle Cluster File System 2) is a shared disk file system developed by Oracle Corporation and released under the GNU General Public License. The original OCFS was not POSIX-compliant. In version 2, POSIX features were included. OCFS2 was integrated as a production filesystem since version 2.6.19 of the Linux kernel. OCFS2 uses a distributed lock manager which resembles the OpenVMS DLM but is much simpler. OCFS2 allows multiple nodes to access the same disk at the same time while behaving like a normal file system. Files, directories are always in sync across all nodes.

nfs

Network File System (NFS) is a distributed file system protocol that allows a user on a client computer to access files over a network as if they were accessing local storage. The Network File System is an open standard defined in RFCs, allowing anyone to implement the protocol.

Perform file system creation, mounting and maintenance

The basic steps in creating a filesystem are

- Locate a hard drive on the system that contains unused space.
- Create a partition on an unused portion of the drive.
- Create the filesystem on the new partition.

The df command can be used to report on current file system disk space usage:

```
[root@matthew pam.d]# df
Filesystem           1K-blocks      Used Available Use% Mounted on
/dev/mapper/vg_matthew-lv_root
                       9845280   5088352   4256808  55% /
tmpfs                   510436       272    510164   1% /dev/shm
/dev/sda1               495844     55619    414625  12% /boot
/dev/sr0               3589186   3589186         0 100%
/mnt/OL6_LOCAL
```

The lsscsi command will list SCSI devices and their attributes. Running that command, shows that there are several drives available:

```
[root@matthew pam.d]# lsscsi
[1:0:0:0]    cd/dvd  VBOX     CD-ROM           1.0   /dev/sr0
[2:0:0:0]    disk    ATA      VBOX HARDDISK    1.0   /dev/sda
[3:0:0:0]    disk    ATA      VBOX HARDDISK    1.0   /dev/sdb
[4:0:0:0]    disk    ATA      VBOX HARDDISK    1.0   /dev/sdc
[5:0:0:0]    disk    ATA      VBOX HARDDISK    1.0   /dev/sdd
```

Before creating a partition on one of the available drives, it is important to check to ensure that it contains free space. Be aware that fdisk is very unforgiving. If you tell it to delete or modify a partition -- it will do so, regardless of how much data might be destroyed. Running fdisk and using the 'p' command shows that this drive has no partitions.

```
[root@matthew ~]# fdisk /dev/sdb

Command (m for help): p

Disk /dev/sdb: 3221 MB, 3221225472 bytes
255 heads, 63 sectors/track, 391 cylinders
Units = cylinders of 16065 * 512 = 8225280 bytes
Sector size (logical/physical): 512 bytes / 512 bytes
I/O size (minimum/optimal): 512 bytes / 512 bytes
Disk identifier: 0xfee0905e

   Device Boot      Start         End      Blocks   Id  System
```

Since there are no partitions, it is possible to create a new one without destroying data. Using the 'n' command starts the Q&A process to create a new partition. The below answers create a primary partition number 1, that uses the entire drive (cylinders 1-391). The 'w' command is then used to write the information out to the drive. Until the 'w' command is executed, nothing is changed on the drive. After it has been executed, there is no turning back!

```
[root@matthew ~]# fdisk /dev/sdb

Command (m for help): n
Command action
   e   extended
   p   primary partition (1-4)
p
Partition number (1-4): 1
First cylinder (1-391, default 1):
Using default value 1
Last cylinder, +cylinders or +size{K,M,G} (1-391, default 391):
Using default value 391

Command (m for help): w
The partition table has been altered!

Calling ioctl() to re-read partition table.
Syncing disks.
```

The partprobe command informs the kernel of partition table changes. You can run this command with the device name as an argument to make the operating system re-read the partition table.

```
[root@matthew ~]# partprobe /dev/sdb
```

Since /dev/sdb now has a partition, running 'fdisk -l' on the /dev/sdb device should list it:

```
[root@matthew ~]# fdisk -l /dev/sdb

Disk /dev/sdb: 3221 MB, 3221225472 bytes
255 heads, 63 sectors/track, 391 cylinders
Units = cylinders of 16065 * 512 = 8225280 bytes
Sector size (logical/physical): 512 bytes / 512 bytes
I/O size (minimum/optimal): 512 bytes / 512 bytes
Disk identifier: 0xfee0905e

   Device Boot      Start         End      Blocks   Id  System
/dev/sdb1               1         391     3140676   83  Linux
```

The Id of 83 means that this is a Linux partition. Since an available partition exists on that drive, there should be a new device available: /dev/sdb1 (sdb partition 1). The next step is to create a file system on that device.

```
[root@matthew ~]# ls /dev/sdb*
/dev/sdb  /dev/sdb1
```

The following example uses the mkfs utility to create an ext4 file system on the /dev/sdb1 device. The command uses the -L option to label the new filesystem 'NewFS'.

```
[root@matthew /]# mkfs -t ext4 -L NewFS /dev/sdb1
mke2fs 1.41.12 (17-May-2010)
Filesystem label=NewFS
OS type: Linux
Block size=4096 (log=2)
Fragment size=4096 (log=2)
Stride=0 blocks, Stripe width=0 blocks
196608 inodes, 785169 blocks
39258 blocks (5.00%) reserved for the super user
```

```
First data block=0
Maximum filesystem blocks=805306368
24 block groups
32768 blocks per group, 32768 fragments per group
8192 inodes per group
Superblock backups stored on blocks:
        32768, 98304, 163840, 229376, 294912

Writing inode tables: done
Creating journal (16384 blocks): done
Writing superblocks and filesystem accounting information: done

This filesystem will be automatically checked every 24 mounts or
180 days, whichever comes first. Use tune2fs -c or -i to override.
```

The file system has been created and can now be mounted. In order to be mounted, a directory needs to be created on the system to serve as the mount point. The mkdir command is used to create the /NewFS directory. After that, the mount command can be used to mount the /dev/sdb1 device on the '/NewFS' directory:

```
[root@matthew /]# mkdir /NewFS
[root@matthew /]# mount /dev/sdb1 /NewFS
```

The df command now displays the new filesystem:

```
[root@matthew /]# df
Filesystem           1K-blocks      Used Available Use% Mounted on
/dev/mapper/vg_matthew-lv_root
                       9845280   3648604   5696556  40% /
tmpfs                   510436       260    510176   1% /dev/shm
/dev/sda1               495844     55619    414625  12% /boot
/dev/sdb1              3091284     70144   2864108   3% /NewFS
```

If the filesystem should be mounted automatically at boot, it must have an entry in the /etc/fstab file. This file contains the mount table information of all the file systems to be mounted when the system is booted. After editing the /etc/fstab and adding a line for the new drive, it will mount automatically on boot:

```
#
# /etc/fstab
# Created by anaconda on Tue Sep 10 13:54:14 2013
#
# Accessible filesystems, by reference, are maintained under '/dev/disk'
# See man pages fstab(5), findfs(8), mount(8) and/or blkid(8) for more info
#
/dev/mapper/vg_matthew-lv_root /                       ext4    defaults        1
 1
UUID=6382ae28-0002-4f85-85b0-fc681e1a3987 /boot                   ext4    defaul
ts        1 2
/dev/mapper/vg_matthew-lv_swap swap                    swap    defaults        0
 0
tmpfs                   /dev/shm                tmpfs   defaults        0 0
devpts                  /dev/pts                devpts  gid=5,mode=620  0 0
sysfs                   /sys                    sysfs   defaults        0 0
proc                    /proc                   proc    defaults        0 0
/dev/sdb1               /NewFS                  ext4    defaults        0 0
```

Manage swap space

Swap space in Linux is used when the amount of physical memory (RAM) runs low and any applications running on the system require additional memory. When this happens, inactive pages in physical RAM are moved to the swap space and the RAM cleared for use by the applications that require it. Swap space is located on hard disk drives. Because drives have a much slower access time than RAM, adding swap space is not a substitute for adding additional RAM to a system. It is best used as a buffer for times when the system is using more memory resources than normal. Systems that must make use of swap space routinely to perform normal functioning will have degraded performance.

Swap space can be a dedicated swap partition, a swap file, or a combination of the two. Of the options, the ideal (best performing) method is to use a dedicated swap partition. The standard recommendation has traditionally been that swap space should be twice the size of the physical RAM. However, this rule originated when the amount of RAM in servers was measured in megabytes. The amount of RAM in high-end servers has been steadily climbing over the years. For servers with more than 2-3GB of RAM, there should be no need to allocate twice that amount in swap space. The amount of swap space required depends on the number, nature, and type of applications among other factors.

Swap partitions are created using any of the available partition editors. Any of the three mentioned earlier: fdisk, parted, or cfdisk can do so. A swap file can be created on a standard file system with the 'dd' command. However, before creating either a swap partition or a swap file, it makes sense to see how much swap space currently exists and how much is being used. The free command displays the swap space.

```
[root@matthew /]# free
             total       used       free     shared    buffers     cached
Mem:       1020876     662240     358636          0      11692     350028
-/+ buffers/cache:     300520     720356
Swap:      2064380         20    2064360
```

From the above, the system is using 20K of swap space and has 2,064,360 K free. Based on that, there does not appear to be a need for more. The swapon -s command provides the same information, and also shows that the swap space is being provided by a partition rather than a swap file.

```
[root@matthew /]# swapon -s
Filename                        Type        Size Used Priority
/dev/dm-1                                   partition 2064380  20   -1
```

Creating a swap partition

Create a partition using a partition editor as described in the previous chapter.

Use the mkswap command to initialize the new partition as a swap space. For a device at /dev/sdc1, the command would be:

```
mkswap /dev/sdc1
```

Enable the new swap space using the swapon command:

```
swapon /dev/sdc1
```

Add the new swap partition to the /etc/fstab file to make it available at boot.

Creating a swap file

Create a swap file using the dd command. The following command creates the file /swapfile of blocksize 1024:

```
[root@matthew /]# dd if=/dev/zero of=/swapfile bs=1024
count=65536
65536+0 records in
65536+0 records out
67108864 bytes (67 MB) copied, 0.256299 s, 262 MB/s

[root@matthew /]# ls -l swapfile
-rw-r--r--. 1 root root 67108864 Sep 11 14:16 swapfile
```

Use the mkswap command to initialize the new file as a swap space.

```
[root@matthew /]# mkswap /swapfile
mkswap: /swapfile: warning: don't erase bootbits sectors
on whole disk. Use -f to force.
Setting up swapspace version 1, size = 65532 KiB
no label, UUID=930dcd5c-bb22-4a82-83c0-c6b25b41fc70
```

Enable the new swap file on the system using the swapon command:

```
[root@matthew /]# swapon /swapfile
```

Use archiving and compression tools like tar, cpio, zip and gzip

Archiving and compression in Linux are two entirely separate functions. Both are used as part of the process of backing up files on a given system.

- **Archival** – This is the process of grouping multiple files together into a single archive file without changing the size of the files.
- **Compression** – This is the act of running a compression algorithm against one or more files that has the effect of reducing the size

of the existing file (or creating a new file that is smaller than the original).

Using these definitions, tar and cpio are archive utilities with no ability to compress files. The gzip utility performs compression with no ability to archive. The zip utility does both, as it can combine multiple files into a single compressed archive.

Both tar and cpio have a single purpose: concatenate many separate files to a single stream. The tar utility tends to be more widely used due to its relative simplicity. It has the ability to use input files as arguments, whereas cpio must be coupled with find. The tar utility is able to search directories on its own and takes the list of files or directories to be backed up from command line arguments. The cpio utility cpio archives only the files or directories it is told to and does not search subdirectories recursively on its own. It also gets the list of items to be archived from stdin, which is why it is almost always used in combination with the find command.

Files are often compressed using ZIP or GZIP in order to save space on the filesystem or to reduce the amount of time needed to transmit files across a network or the Internet. GZIP generally surpasses ZIP in terms of compression, especially when compressing a huge number of files. However, ZIP is capable of both archiving and compressing the files simultaneously. GZIP is often used in combination with TAR to perform both compression and archiving. When using the ZIP utility, the original file(s) are left unchanged, and a new compressed archive file is created. The GZIP utility compresses the original file and adds a .gz extension to it.

Some of the common commands for the four utilities follow:

TAR

Create an archive.

```
# cd /tmp
# tar -cvf archive_file.tar archive-dir
```

Check the contents.

```
# tar -tvf /tmp/archive_file.tar
```

Extract it.

```
# cd /tmp/extract-dir
# tar -xvf /tmp/archive_file.tar
```

CPIO

Create an archive.

```
# cd /tmp
# find archive_dir | cpio -ov > archive_file.cpio
```

Check the contents.

```
# cpio -t < /tmp/archive_file.cpio
```

Extract it.

```
# cd /tmp/extract-dir
# cpio -idmv < /tmp/archive_file.cpio
```

ZIP

Create an archive.

```
# cd /tmp
# zip -r archive_file.zip archive_dir
```

Check the contents.

```
# unzip -l archive_file.zip
```

Extract it.

```
# cd /tmp/extract-dir
# unzip /tmp/archive_file.zip
```

GZIP

Compress the specified file giving it a ".gz" extension.

```
# cd /tmp
# tar -cvf archive_file.tar archive_dir
# gzip archive_file.tar
```

The "-z" option of the tar command allows you to do this directly.

```
# cd /tmp
# tar -cvzf archive_file.tar.gz archive_dir
```

Uncompress the file.

```
# gunzip archive_file.tar.gz
```

The "-z" option of the tar command allows you to directly ungzip and extract a ".tar.gz" file.

```
# cd /tmp/extract-dir
# tar -xvzf /tmp/archive_file.tar.gz
```

Describe ASMLib package

Automatic Storage Management (ASM) is a volume manager and a file system for Oracle database files. ASM is Oracle's recommended storage management solution. It provides an alternative to conventional volume managers, file systems, and raw devices. ASM simplifies database administration and significantly reduces kernel resource usage. By requiring only the management of groups of disks allocated to the Oracle Database, ASM eliminates the need for the DBA to directly manage potentially thousands of Oracle database files

ASMLib is an optional support library that allows an Oracle Database using ASM more efficient and capable access to the disk groups it is using. The ASMLib software consists of three components:

- **Oracle ASMLib kernel driver** -- included in UEK
- **Oracleasm-support package** -- available from ULN
- **Oracleasmlib package** -- available from ULN

Describe Clusterware add-on package

Oracle Clusterware is portable cluster software that enables servers to communicate with each other, so that they appear to function as a collective unit. Combining servers in this fashion is commonly known as a cluster. Each server has additional processes that allow them to communicate with the other servers in the cluster. When combined in this fashion, the separate servers appear as if they are a single system to applications and end users.

Oracle Clusterware provides the infrastructure necessary to run Oracle Real Application Clusters (Oracle RAC). Oracle Clusterware can be programmed to manage the availability of user applications and Oracle databases. It can manage all of the resources automatically in an Oracle RAC environment. Oracle Clusterware is required for using Oracle RAC and is the only clusterware needed for platforms on which Oracle RAC operates. Oracle RAC continues to support many third-party clusterware products on specific platforms. However, you must also install and use Oracle Clusterware.

Oracle Clusterware is capable of protecting any kind of application in a failover cluster. Oracle Linux Support customers at the Basic or Premier level are now entitled, at no additional license and support costs, to download and deploy Oracle Clusterware in a Linux cluster covered under their Oracle Linux Support agreement. This provides customers with the ability to enable applications running in the cluster to be monitored and managed by Oracle Clusterware for high availability.

Network Administration

Describe network interface configuration files

The /etc/sysconfig/network-scripts/ contains the configuration files for network interfaces. The directory also contains the scripts used to activate and deactivate these network interfaces. There are three categories of files that exist in this directory:

- Interface configuration files
- Interface control scripts
- Network function files

The primary network configuration files on Oracle Linux systems are:

- **/etc/hosts** -- The main purpose of this file is to resolve hostnames that cannot be resolved any other way. It can also be used to resolve hostnames on small networks with no DNS server. Regardless of the type of network the computer is on, this file should contain a line specifying the IP address of the loopback device (127.0.0.1) as localhost.localdomain.
- **/etc/resolv.conf** -- This file specifies the IP addresses of DNS servers and the search domain. Unless configured to do otherwise, the network initialization scripts populate this file.
- **/etc/sysconfig/network** -- This file specifies routing and host information for all network interfaces.
- **/etc/sysconfig/network-scripts/ifcfg-interface-name** -- For each network interface, there is a corresponding interface configuration script. Each of these files provide information specific to a particular network interface.
- **/etc/sysconfig/networking/** -- This directory is used by the Network Administration Tool and its contents should not be edited manually.
- **/etc/nsswitch.conf** -- This is the Name Service Switch (NSS) configuration file and is used by the GNU C Library to determine the sources (NIS, DNS, files) from which to obtain name-service information in a range of categories, and in what order.

Interface Configuration Files:

These control the software interfaces for individual network devices. The files are used during the system boot process to determine what interfaces to bring up and how to configure them. The files are usually named ifcfg-name, where name refers to the name of the device that the configuration file controls. One of the most common is /etc/sysconfig/network-scripts/ifcfg-eth0. This file controls the first Ethernet network interface card or NIC in the system. In a system with multiple Ethernet cards, there are multiple ifcfg-eth# files. Each device has its own file and can be configured individually.

Interface control scripts

Interface control scripts activate and deactivate system interfaces. There are two primary interface control scripts that call on control scripts located in the /etc/sysconfig/network-scripts/ directory: /sbin/ifdown and /sbin/ifup. The ifup and ifdown interface scripts are symbolic links to scripts in the /sbin/ directory. When calling either ifup or ifdown, they require the value of the interface to be specified, such as:

```
ifup eth0
```

The easiest way to manipulate all network scripts simultaneously is to use the /sbin/service command on the network service (/etc/rc.d/init.d/network), with a command in the format of "/sbin/service network action". The action can be either status, start, stop, or restart. To view a list of configured devices and currently active network interfaces, use the following command:

```
/sbin/service network status
```

Network function files

Oracle Linux 6 has several files that contain important common functions used to bring interfaces up and down. Rather than forcing each interface control file to contain these functions, they are grouped together in a few files. The /etc/sysconfig/network-scripts/network-functions file contains the most commonly used IPv4 functions, which are useful to many interface control scripts. These functions include contacting running programs that have requested information about changes in the status of an interface, setting hostnames, finding a gateway device, verifying whether or not a particular device is down, and adding a default route.

As the functions required for IPv6 interfaces are different from IPv4 interfaces, a /etc/sysconfig/network-scripts/network-functions-ipv6 file exists specifically to hold this information. The functions in this file configure and delete static IPv6 routes, create and remove tunnels, add and remove IPv6 addresses to an interface, and test for the existence of an IPv6 address on an interface.

Use command line network interface utilities

The ifconfig utility has long been the tool of choice to check the status of network interfaces as well as configuring them. When executed with no arguments, ifconfig displays the status of the currently active interfaces. If a single interface argument is supplied, ifconfig displays the status of the given interface only. When executed with the -a argument, it displays the status of all interfaces, even those that are down. The example below shows information for the eth0 and lo interfaces. The eth0 interface corresponds to the first Ethernet NIC configured on this system. In that section is the hardware address, IP address, broadcast address, netmask, status (UP), and transmit/receive packets, errors etc.

```
[root@matthew /]# ifconfig
eth0      Link encap:Ethernet  HWaddr 08:00:27:10:48:54
          inet addr:192.201.200.23  Bcast:192.201.200.255
Mask:255.255.255.0
          inet6 addr: fe80::a00:27ff:fe10:4854/64 Scope:Link
          UP BROADCAST RUNNING MULTICAST  MTU:1500  Metric:1
          RX packets:277797 errors:0 dropped:0 overruns:0 frame:0
          TX packets:186357 errors:0 dropped:0 overruns:0 carrier:0
          collisions:0 txqueuelen:1000
          RX bytes:300812741 (286.8 MiB)  TX bytes:10089923 (9.6 MiB)

lo        Link encap:Local Loopback
          inet addr:127.0.0.1  Mask:255.0.0.0
          inet6 addr: ::1/128 Scope:Host
          UP LOOPBACK RUNNING  MTU:16436  Metric:1
          RX packets:48 errors:0 dropped:0 overruns:0 frame:0
          TX packets:48 errors:0 dropped:0 overruns:0 carrier:0
          collisions:0 txqueuelen:0
          RX bytes:3230 (3.1 KiB)  TX bytes:3230 (3.1 KiB)
```

That said, the ifconfig command is soon going to become obsolete. The ip command serves a similar purpose. It has the ability to display and manipulate routing, devices, policy routing and tunnels. Executing the command 'ip link' will show you the network devices configuration:

```
[root@matthew /]# ip link
1: lo: <LOOPBACK,UP,LOWER_UP> mtu 16436 qdisc noqueue state UNKNOWN
    link/loopback 00:00:00:00:00:00 brd 00:00:00:00:00:00
2: eth0: <BROADCAST,MULTICAST,UP,LOWER_UP> mtu 1500 qdisc pfifo_fast
state UP qlen 1000
```

The 'ip addr' command will display the IP address information:

```
[root@matthew /]# ip addr
1: lo: <LOOPBACK,UP,LOWER_UP> mtu 16436 qdisc noqueue state UNKNOWN
    link/loopback 00:00:00:00:00:00 brd 00:00:00:00:00:00
    inet 127.0.0.1/8 scope host lo
    inet6 ::1/128 scope host
       valid_lft forever preferred_lft forever
2: eth0: <BROADCAST,MULTICAST,UP,LOWER_UP> mtu 1500 qdisc pfifo_fast
state UP qlen 1000
    link/ether 08:00:27:10:48:54 brd ff:ff:ff:ff:ff:ff
    inet 192.201.200.23/24 brd 192.201.200.255 scope global eth0
    inet6 fe80::a00:27ff:fe10:4854/64 scope link
       valid_lft forever preferred_lft forever
```

As mentioned in the previous section, the interface control scripts activate and deactivate system interfaces. Two of the primary interface control scripts that call on control scripts are 'ifdown' and 'ifup'. Executing 'ifdown eth0' will deactivate the 'eth0' interface. Executing the 'ip addr' command for the eth0 interface, shows no IP assigned to the card, indicating it is inactive.

```
[root@matthew /]# ifdown eth0
Device state: 3 (disconnect

[root@matthew /]# ip addr show eth0
2: eth0: <BROADCAST,MULTICAST,UP,LOWER_UP> mtu 1500 qdisc pfifo_fast
state UP qlen 1000
    link/ether 08:00:27:10:48:54 brd ff:ff:ff:ff:ff:ff
    inet6 fe80::a00:27ff:fe10:4854/64 scope link
       valid_lft forever preferred_lft forever
```

Executing 'ifup eth0' will re-activate it. Executing the ip addr command for the eth0 interface shows that the card now has an IP assigned again.

```
[root@matthew /]# ifup eth0
Active connection state: activating
Active connection path:
/org/freedesktop/NetworkManager/ActiveConnection/17
state: activated
Connection activated
[root@matthew /]# ip addr show eth0
2: eth0: <BROADCAST,MULTICAST,UP,LOWER_UP> mtu 1500 qdisc pfifo_fast
state UP qlen 1000
    link/ether 08:00:27:10:48:54 brd ff:ff:ff:ff:ff:ff
    inet 10.0.2.15/24 brd 10.0.2.255 scope global eth0
    inet6 fe80::a00:27ff:fe10:4854/64 scope link
       valid_lft forever preferred_lft forever
```

The ethtool utility allows you to configure Network Interface Cards (NICs). With it you can query and change settings such as speed, duplex mode, port, auto-negotiation, and PCI locations on many network devices. Executing 'ethtool eth0' displays the following information about the eth0 NIC:

```
[root@matthew /]# ethtool eth0
Settings for eth0:
    Supported ports: [ TP ]
    Supported link modes:   10baseT/Half 10baseT/Full
                            100baseT/Half 100baseT/Full
                            1000baseT/Full
    Supports auto-negotiation: Yes
    Advertised link modes:  10baseT/Half 10baseT/Full
                            100baseT/Half 100baseT/Full
                            1000baseT/Full
    Advertised pause frame use: No
    Advertised auto-negotiation: Yes
    Speed: 1000Mb/s
    Duplex: Full
    Port: Twisted Pair
    PHYAD: 0
    Transceiver: internal
    Auto-negotiation: on
    MDI-X: Unknown
    Supports Wake-on: umbg
    Wake-on: d
    Current message level: 0x00000007 (7)
    Link detected: yes
```

The ethtool utility can also be used to configure the card. The following example sets the eth0 NIC to 100BaseT and full duplex:

```
ethtool -s eth0 speed 100 duplex full
```

The ‘service' command can be used to check status, stop, start, or restart various services on the system. In the below example, it is used to check the network status. The output shows that there are two interfaces (eth0 and lo) configured and that both are active.

```
[root@matthew /]# service network status
Configured devices:
lo eth0
Currently active devices:
lo eth0
```

The 'netstat' command in conjunction with ‘ip route' is often used to resolve network routing issues. Netstat can be used to display network connections, routing tables, interface statistics, masquerade connections, and multicast memberships. The ‘ip route' command allows you to manipulate the routing on your system. The specifics of network routing are complex and go well beyond this guide.

Use the NetworkManager tool to configure network connections

NetworkManager is a network control and configuration application. Its purpose is to keep network devices and connections up and active when they are available. It consists of a core daemon and a GNOME Notification Area applet that provides network status information, and configuration tools for creating, editing and removing connections and interfaces.

NetworkManager can be used to configure some of the following types of connections: Ethernet, wireless, mobile broadband (such as cellular 3G), and DSL and PPPoE (Point-to-Point over Ethernet). NetworkManager can also assist with configuration of network aliases, static routes, DNS information and VPN connections. NetworkManager should be installed by default on Oracle Linux 6 systems.

NetworkManager's Notification Area applet allows you to perform network configuration tasks. If the NetworkManager package is installed and the applet is running, the applet icon will be available in the GNOME panel. The following ps command verfies that the applet is running:

```
[root@matthew /]# ps -ef | grep nm-applet
root      2580  2371  0 10:31 ?        00:00:00 nm-applet --sm-
disable
root      7456  2886  0 19:18 pts/0    00:00:00 grep nm-a
```

The NetworkManager applet icon is the second one from the left in the below image (i.e. the two offset PCs). This indicates a Wired Network connection that is enabled. If it is not running, it can be started by executing 'nm-applet &' from the command line.

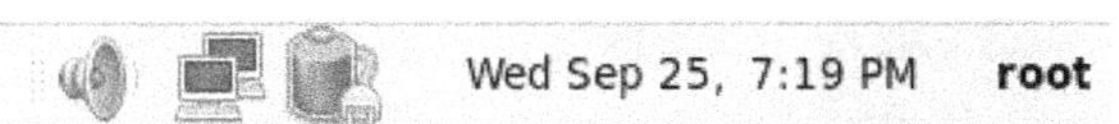

Right-clicking on the NetworkManager applet icon will open an options screen. From the screen, it is possible to enable networking, enable notifications, see connection information, and edit connections using this applet.

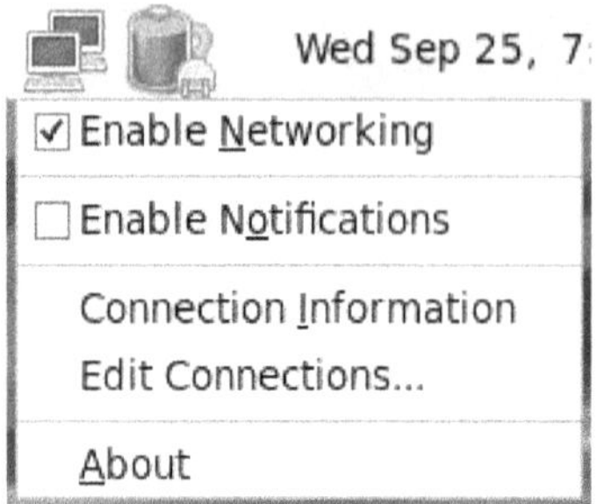

Selecting the connection information from the options screen opens the Connection Information window. It will contain information similar to the screenshot below. You can find the Interface name, speed, IP address, DNS server information etc. in this window for your network connection.

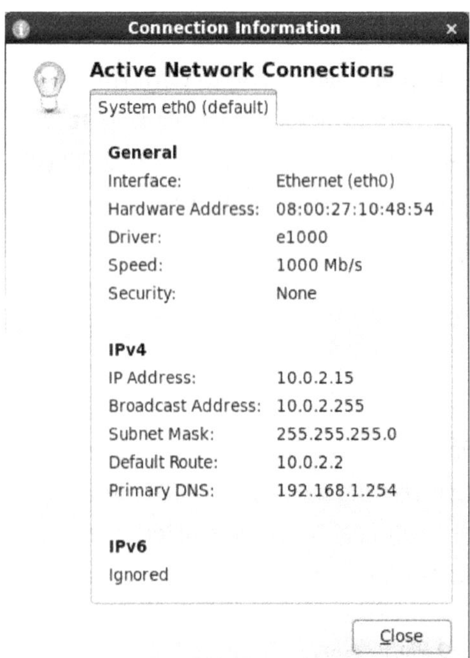

To edit the network connections, you can right click the NetworkManager applet icon and then select the Edit Connections option. This will launch the Network Connections window. This window displays the names of all network interfaces on your system. The example below displays the 'System eth0' network interface.

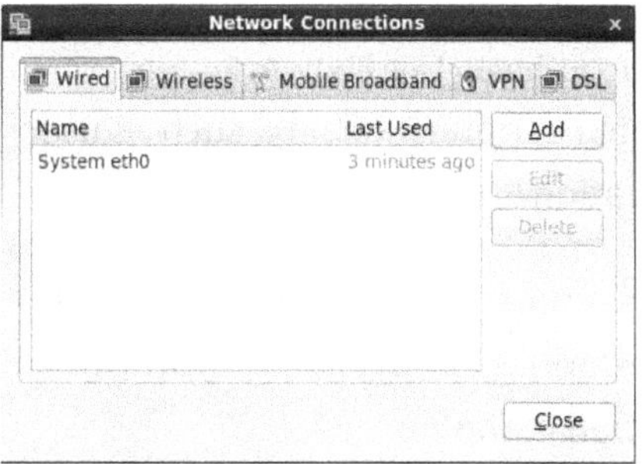

Selecting a given network interface and clicking the Edit button will open the Edit window. In this window it is possible to see and alter the network interface parameters that can be modified, such as the MTU size, IPv4 settings, IPv6 settings, and more. From this window, it is also possible to set the 'Connect automatically' flag. When set, the system will establish the network connection automatically for this selected network interface during the system boot. If left unchecked, the connection must be enabled manually via the NetworkManager applet's left-click menu after every reboot of the system.

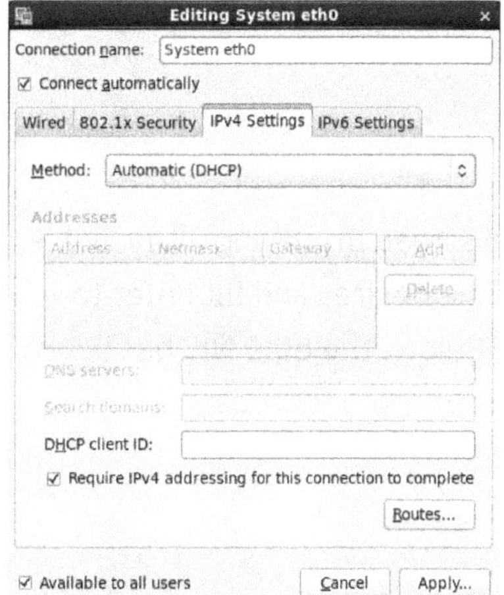

Use the system-config-network utility

NetworkManager is the recommended and preferred utility for configuring the network interface with Oracle Linux 6. However, prior releases of Oracle Linux made use of the Network Administration Tool. The Network Administration Tool is commonly referred to as the 'system-config-network' tool after its command line invocation. In both Oracle Linux 6 and in RHEL 6, NetworkManager replaces the Network Administration Tool. It also provides enhanced functionality, such as user specific and mobile broadband configuration.

Even though NetworkManager is the recommended option, the Network Administration Tool (system-config-network) is still available in Oracle Linux 6. It stores configuration information in the '/etc/sysconfig/networking/' directory. The contents of this directory should not be edited manually. Invoking the utility from the command line brings up the opening screen:

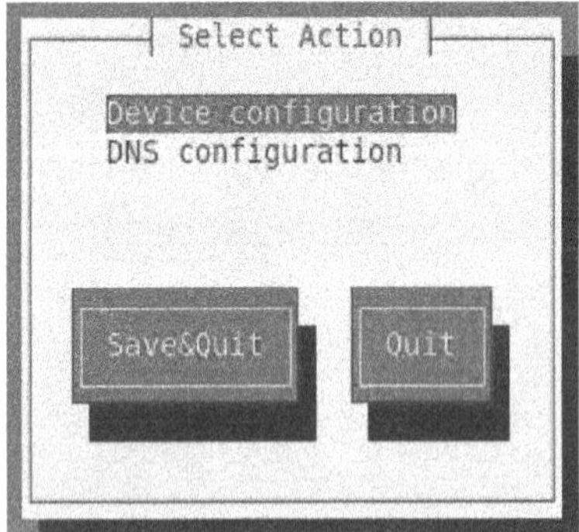

Selecting 'Device Configuration' brings up a screen displaying all available devices. From there, you can select one of the devices and hit enter to open a screen allowing you to configure it. Below, the eth0 NIC has been selected:

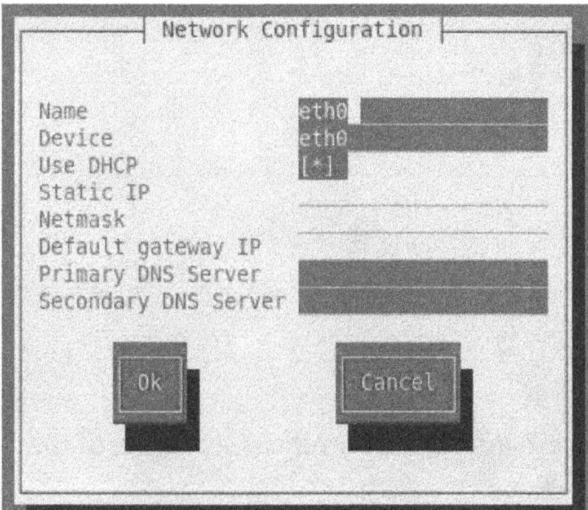

Alternately, selecting 'DNS Configuration' from the main screen will allow you to configure your Domain Name System:

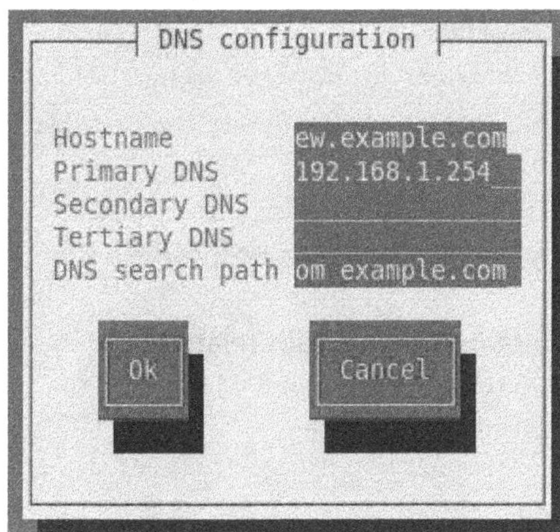

Examine files in /etc/sysconfig/network-scripts

The files in the /etc/sysconfig/network-scripts are interface control scripts that activate and deactivate system interfaces. It also contains configuration files for network interfaces. Below is a screenshot showing the files in this directory:

```
[root@matthew /]# cd /etc/sysconfig/network-scripts/
[root@matthew network-scripts]# ls
ifcfg-eth0   ifdown-post    ifup-eth     ifup-routes
ifcfg-lo     ifdown-ppp     ifup-ippp    ifup-sit
ifdown       ifdown-routes  ifup-ipv6    ifup-tunnel
ifdown-bnep  ifdown-sit     ifup-isdn    ifup-wireless
ifdown-eth   ifdown-tunnel  ifup-plip    init.ipv6-global
ifdown-ippp  ifup           ifup-plusb   net.hotplug
ifdown-ipv6  ifup-aliases   ifup-post    network-functions
ifdown-isdn  ifup-bnep      ifup-ppp     network-functions-ipv6
```

The majority of the files shown are interface control scripts. Some of the more commonly used scripts include:

- **ifup-aliases** -- Configures IP aliases from interface configuration files when more than one IP address is associated with an interface.
- **ifup-ippp** and **ifdown-ippp** -- Brings ISDN interfaces up and down.
- **ifup-ipv6** and **ifdown-ipv6** -- Brings IPv6 interfaces up and down.
- **ifup-plip** -- Brings up a PLIP interface.
- **ifup-plusb** -- Brings up a USB interface for network connections.
- **ifup-post** and **ifdown-post** -- Contains commands to be executed after an interface is brought up or down.
- **ifup-ppp** and **ifdown-ppp** -- Brings a PPP interface up or down.
- **ifup-routes** -- Adds static routes for a device as its interface is brought up.
- **ifdown-sit** and **ifup-sit** -- Contains function calls related to bringing up and down an IPv6 tunnel within an IPv4 connection.
- **ifup-wireless** -- Brings up a wireless interface.

You will also find the 'ifcfg-eth0' file in the directory. This is the configuration file which controls the first Ethernet network interface card (NIC) in the system. Each device has its own configuration file. In a system with multiple NICs, there are multiple ifcfg-ethX files (where X is a unique number corresponding to a specific interface). An example of an 'ifcfg-eth0' is below:

```
DEVICE="eth0"
BOOTPROTO="dhcp"
NM_CONTROLLED="yes"
ONBOOT=yes
TYPE="Ethernet"
UUID="94dcb51e-7fe6-4c44-991c-497690f2542e"
HWADDR=08:00:27:10:48:54
DEFROUTE=yes
PEERDNS=yes
PEERROUTES=yes
IPV4_FAILURE_FATAL=yes
IPV6INIT=no
NAME="System eth0"
LAST_CONNECT=1378838016
```

The ifcfg-lo file is the local loopback interface file.

```
DEVICE=lo
IPADDR=127.0.0.1
NETMASK=255.0.0.0
NETWORK=127.0.0.0
# If you're having problems with gated making 127.0.0.0/8 a martian,
# you can change this to something else (255.255.255.255, for
example)
BROADCAST=127.255.255.255
ONBOOT=yes
NAME=loopback
```

Set up bonding

Oracle Linux allows administrators to bind multiple network interfaces together into a single channel using the bonding kernel module and a special network interface called a channel bonding interface. Channel bonding enables two or more network interfaces to act as one. Bonding network interfaces in this fashion simultaneously increase the bandwidth and provides redundancy.

The first step in making a channel bonding interface is to create a file in the /etc/sysconfig/network-scripts/ directory. The file should be called ifcfg-bondX, where X is the number for the interface, such as 0. The file contents can be identical to the type of interface being bonded, such as an Ethernet interface. The only required difference is that the DEVICE directive be bondX, where X is the number for the interface. Any desired parameters for the bonding kernel module must be specified as a space-separated list in the BONDING_OPTS directive in the interface file.

A sample channel bonding configuration file follows:

```
DEVICE=bond0
IPADDR=192.168.1.1
NETMASK=255.255.255.0
ONBOOT=yes
BOOTPROTO=none
USERCTL=no
BONDING_OPTS="mode=0 miimon=1000"
```

In the above file, the device name is ‘bond0’. An IP address and netmask value are assigned to the bonding interface. The ONBOOT=yes parameter means this interface will be activated at boot time. In BONDING_OPTS parameter, the mode and miimon values are specified. The mode allows you to specify the bonding policy. The miimon value specifies how often MII link monitoring occurs in milliseconds.

The possible bonding modes are:

- **0** — (balance-rr) Sets a round-robin policy for fault tolerance and load balancing.
- **1** — (active-backup) Sets an active-backup policy for fault tolerance.
- **2** — (balance-xor) Sets an XOR (exclusive-or) policy for fault tolerance and load balancing.
- **3** — (broadcast) Sets a broadcast policy for fault tolerance.
- **5** — (balance-tlb) Sets a Transmit Load Balancing (TLB) policy for fault tolerance and load balancing.
- **6** — (balance-alb) Sets an Active Load Balancing (ALB) policy for fault tolerance and load balancing.

Once the channel bonding interface has been created, the network interfaces to be bound together must be configured. Their configuration files must have MASTER and SLAVE directives added to them. The configuration files for each of the channel-bonded interfaces can be

For systems that have multiple network interfaces, there should also be an entry specifying which interface should be used:

```
GATEWAY=192.0.2.1
GATEWAYDEV=eth0
```

You must restart the network service after making any changes to '/etc/sysconfig/network' in order for them to take effect:

```
[root@matthew ~]# service network restart
```

The ip route show command can be used to display the routing table:

```
[root@matthew ~]# ip route show
default via 10.0.3.2 dev eth1  proto static
10.0.3.0/24 dev eth1  proto kernel  scope link  src 10.0.3.15  metric
```

This example shows that packets destined for the local network (10.0.3.0/24) do not use the gateway. The default entry means that any packets destined for addresses outside the local network are routed via the gateway 10.0.3.2. You can also use the netstat -rn command to display this information:

```
[root@matthew ~]# netstat -rn
Kernel IP routing table
Destination  Gateway   Genmask        Flags  MSS Window  irtt Iface
0.0.0.0      10.0.2.2  0.0.0.0        UG       0 0          0 eth0
10.0.2.0     0.0.0.0   255.255.255.0  U        0 0          0 eth0
169.254.0.0  0.0.0.0   255.255.0.0    U        0 0          0 eth0
```

The route command can also be used to display gateway and routing information:

```
[root@matthew etc]# route
Kernel IP routing table
Destination  Gateway   Genmask        Flags Metric Ref    Use Iface
default      10.0.2.2  0.0.0.0        UG    0      0        0 eth0
10.0.2.0     *         255.255.255.0  U     1      0        0 eth0
```

To add or delete a route from the table, use the ip route add or ip route del commands. For example, to replace the entry for the static default route:

```
[root@matthew ~]# ip route del default
[root@matthew ~]# ip route show
10.0.3.0/24 dev eth0 proto kernel scope link src 10.0.3.15

[root@matthew ~]# ip ro add default via 10.0.3.1 dev eth0 proto
static
[root@matthew ~]# ip route show
10.0.3.0/24 dev eth0 proto kernel scope link src 10.0.3.15
default via 10.0.3.1 dev eth0 proto static
```

Changes made to the routing table using ip route are not persistent across system reboots. To permanently configure static routes, you must create a route-interface file in /etc/sysconfig/network-scripts for the interface. An entry in these files can take the same format as the arguments to the ip route add command. Changes made to a route-interface file will not take effect until you restart either the network service or the interface.

Basic Security Administration

Describe SELinux modes, policies, booleans, and contexts

Security-Enhanced Linux (SELinux) is an implementation of a Mandatory Access Control (MAC) mechanism in the Linux kernel. It checks for allowed operations after standard Discretionary Access Controls (DAC) are checked. SELinux was created by the National Security Agency and can enforce rules on files and processes, and on their actions, based on defined policies.

Under SELinux, files (including directories and devices) are referred to as objects. Processes, such as a user running a command or the Mozilla Firefox application, are referred to as subjects. Linux (and most OSs) uses a Discretionary Access Control (DAC) system. It controls how subjects interact with objects, and how subjects interact with each other. Under DAC, users control the permissions of files (objects) that they own. Under Linux, users could make their home directories world-readable, giving users and processes (subjects) access to potentially sensitive information. Nothing in DAC provides any further protection over this unwanted action and relying on it is inadequate for strong system security.

DAC access decisions are only based on user identity and ownership. Other security-relevant information such as the role of the user, the function and trustworthiness of the program, and the sensitivity and integrity of the data are not taken into account. Users generally have full discretion over their files, making it difficult to enforce a system-wide security policy. In addition programs executed by a user inherit the permissions granted to the user. They can change use those permissions to change access to the user's files, so minimal protection is provided against malicious software.

Security-Enhanced Linux (SELinux) adds Mandatory Access Control (MAC) to the Linux kernel. When properly implemented, SeLinux enables a system to adequately defend itself. It improves application security by protecting secured applications from being tampered with or bypassed.

MAC provides strong separation of applications that permits the safe execution of untrustworthy applications. Limiting the privileges of processes being executed limits the scope of potential damage that can result from the exploitation of vulnerabilities.

SELinux can also provide a Role-Based Access Control (RBAC) security model. In this model, a role acts as an intermediary abstraction layer between SELinux process domains or file types and an SELinux user. Processes run in specific SELinux domains, and file system objects are assigned SELinux file types. SELinux users are authorized to perform specified roles, and roles.

SELinux can run in three different modes:

- **Enforcing** -- SELinux policy is enforced. SELinux denies access based on SELinux policy rules.
- **Permissive** -- SELinux policy is not enforced. SELinux does not deny access, but denials are logged for actions that would have been denied if running in enforcing mode.
- **Disabled** -- SELinux is disabled. Only DAC rules are used.

There are two policies that can be used with SELinux:

- **Targeted** -- This is the default SELinux policy used in Oracle Linux 6. When using targeted policy, processes that are targeted run in a confined domain, and processes that are not targeted run in an unconfined domain. By default, subjects running in an unconfined domain can not allocate writeable memory and execute it. This reduces vulnerability to buffer overflow attacks. These memory checks can be disabled by setting Booleans, which allow the SELinux policy to be modified at runtime. Almost every service that listens on a network, such as sshd or httpd, is confined in Oracle Linux 6. When a process is confined, it runs in its own domain. If a confined process is compromised by an attacker, an attacker's access to resources and the possible damage they can do is limited.

- **Multi-Level Security (MLS)** -- This is a security scheme that enforces the Bell-La Padula Mandatory Access Model. Under MLS, users and processes are called subjects, and files, devices, and other passive components of the system are called objects. Both subjects and objects are labeled with a security level, which entails a subject's clearance or an object's classification. Each security level is composed of a sensitivity and a category, for example, an internal release schedule is filed under the internal documents category with a confidential sensitivity.

Booleans allow parts of SELinux policy to be changed at runtime, without any knowledge of SELinux policy writing. This allows changes, such as allowing services access to NFS file systems, without reloading or recompiling SELinux policy. For a list of Booleans, an explanation of what each one is, and whether they are on or off, run the 'semanage boolean -l' command as the Linux root user. There are dozens of Booleans that can be configured. An example of one is ftp_home_dir. By default this is set to off. Setting the Boolean to on would allow ftp to read and write files in the user home directories.

Enable and disable SELinux configuration

It is possible to check the status of SELinux on an Oracle Linux 6 system using the 'sestatus' command as shown below. In the example below, SELinux is enabled, set to enforcing mode and is using the targeted policy.

```
[root@matthew ~]# sestatus
SELinux status:                 enabled
SELinuxfs mount:                /selinux
Current mode:                   enforcing
Mode from config file:          enforcing
Policy version:                 26
Policy from config file:        target
```

The 'getenforce' command is another way to determine the status of SELinux. It returns only the current mode of SELinux, Enforcing, Permissive, or Disabled. In the example shown below, the 'getenforce' command returns enforcing which means SELinux is enabled on this system and enforcing the security policy.

```
[root@matthew ~]# /usr/sbin/getenforce
Enforcing
```

The SELinux Management GUI allows you to enable, disable, and configure SELinux. It can be launched from the GUI via the System -> Administration -> SELinux Management menu option. Alternately, you can execute 'system-config-selinux' to launch the SELinux GUI application from the command line. You can disable SELinux by setting the System Default Enforcing Mode to 'Disabled' from this utility. You must reboot for the change to take effect.

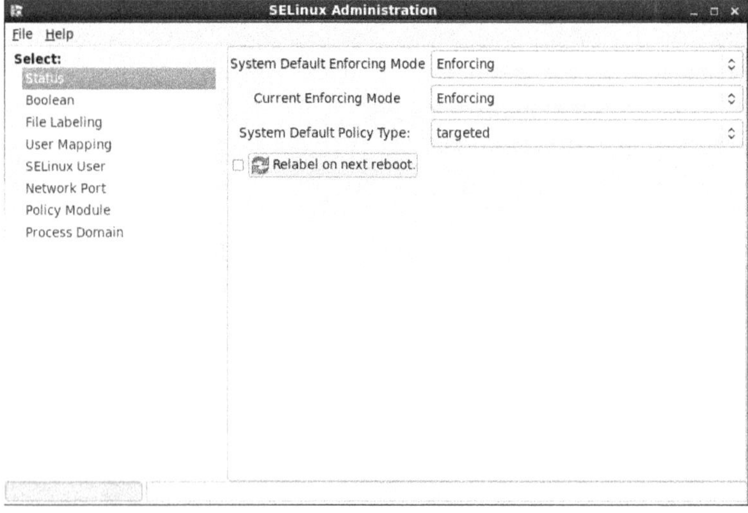

It is also possible to disable SELinux by editing the '/etc/selinux/config' file manually. Open this file with a text editor and change set 'SELINUX=disabled'. Save the file and reboot the system.

Manage access to system services using Service configuration tool

One of the methods for helping to assure the security of your Oracle Linux system is by managing access to system services. There are different ways to manage access to services, but the easiest is to turn the service off. The Service Configuration tool can configure the services managed by 'xinetd' as well as the services in the '/etc/rc.d/init.d' hierarchy. It is a graphical tool that makes it simple to enable and disable services. It can also start, stop, and restart services as needed. The utility can be started from the command line with the command 'system-config-services. It can also be started from the GUI: System -> Administration ->Services menu.

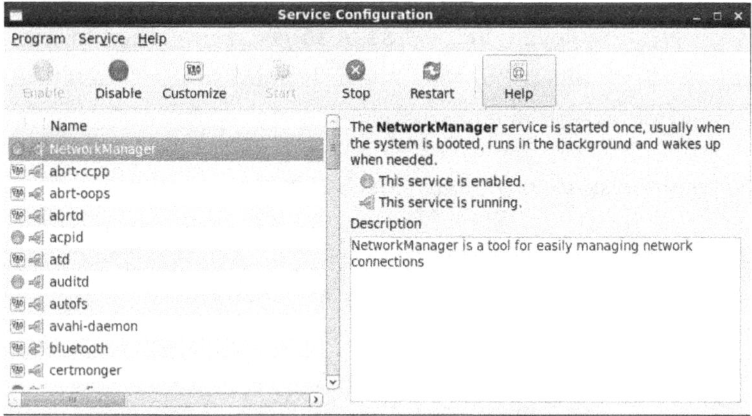

Im the image above, NetworkManager is selected, and it is clear that the service is both enabled and running. Icons along the top of the Service Configuration tool allow the service to be disabled, stopped, restarted, or customized. Clicking the 'Customize' button pulls up another window that allows you to configure which runlevels the service is enabled in:

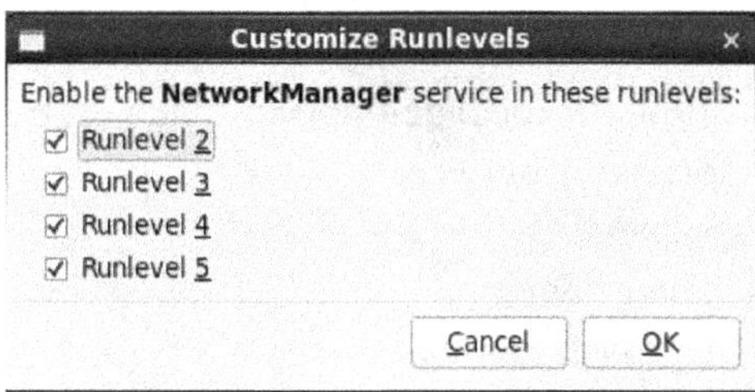

You can click on the name of the service from the list on the left-hand side of the application to select it. Once a service has been selected, Service configuration tool will display a brief description of that service as well as the status. For SysV services, the status window also shows whether they are currently running.

To start, stop, or restart the service immediately, click the appropriate button on the toolbar. Alternately you can choose the action from the Service pull down menu. For xinetd services, the action buttons are disabled because they cannot be started or stopped individually.

To enable a service, select it in the list and click on one of the Enable, Disable buttons. For SysV services, you can also click the Customize button to change the default runlevels. In the case of a SysV service, the runlevel configuration will be changed, but the runlevel is not restarted. Therefore, the changes will not take place immediately.

Some of the common services available on Linux systems include:

- **acpid** -- Advanced Configuration and Power Interface daemon
- **atd** -- Run commands scheduled by at command
- **auditd** -- Linux auditing system daemon
- **autofs** -- Auto-mount file systems on demand
- **bluetooth** -- Trigger bluetoothd start-up
- **crond** -- Service to run scheduled commands via crond daemon
- **cups** -- Common Unix printing system service
- **ip6tables** -- IPv6 IPtables firewall service
- **iptables** -- IPv4 IPtables firewall service
- **kdump** -- Helps loading kdump kernel into memory
- **lvm2-monitor** -- Monitors LVM2 disk volumes
- **network** -- Bring up/down networking on a system
- **nfs** -- This service provides the NFS server functionality
- **ntpd** -- Ntpd is the Network Time Protocol daemon to synch time
- **postfix** -- Postfix mail transport agent service
- **rsyslog** -- Rsyslog logging service
- **sshd** -- Starts the OpenSSH server daemon
- **ypbind** -- NIS daemon running on NIS clients

Use the Firewall configuration tool

In prior releases of Linux a packages called ipchains was used to implement network security. However, it had several shortcomings and the Netfilter organization decided to create a new product called 'iptables'. The iptables package is generally considered to be both faster and more secure than ipchains and is the default firewall package installed under RHEL 6 and Oracle Linux 6 releases.

Firewalls are one of the primary components in a network security implementation. Firewalls are designed to prevent unauthorized access to or from a private network. Their function is to prevent unauthorized network packets from accessing the system's network interface. The firewall examines network traffic and uses a set of rules to allow or deny it access to the network. Requests that are made to a port that is blocked by a firewall are ignored. Any services inside the firewall listening on those ports will never receive any packets. Firewalls that are incorrectly configured are a major cause of 'malfunctioning' services. You must be careful to block ports that are not being used and open ones that are required for the services configured on your system.

On Oracle Linux 6 systems, there is a graphical firewall configuration tool that allows for simple firewall rules to be created. The Firewall Configuration Tool (system-config-firewall) creates basic iptables rules for a general-purpose firewall. If there is a need for more complex rules, advanced users and server administrators need to manually configure the firewall with the 'iptables' command-line utility.

The Firewall Configuration Tool can be started from the menu by selecting System -> Administration -> Firewall. It can also be started by executing 'system-config-firewall' from the command line. The following screenshot shows that the Firewall is enabled on this system. The options at the top have a 'Disable' option and the bottom right has a notice: "The firewall is enabled."

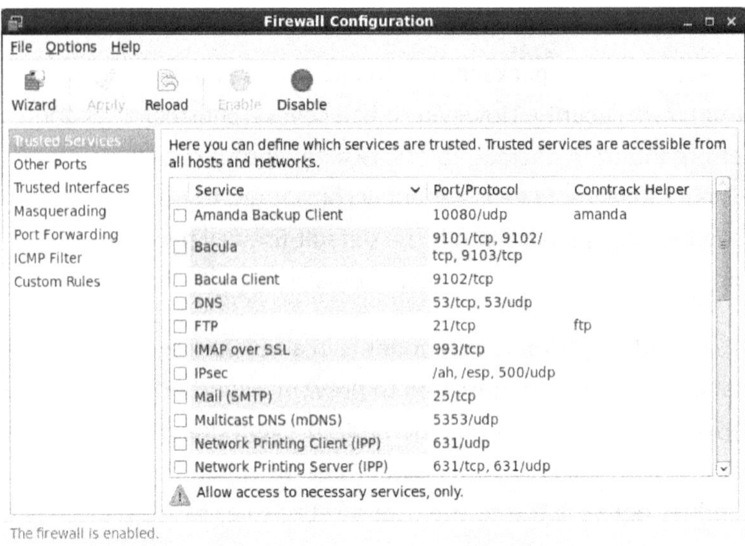

The rules that configure the firewall behavior are stored in the '/etc/sysconfig/iptables' file. The contents of the file will look something like the following:

```
[root@matthew ~]# cat /etc/sysconfig/iptables
# Firewall configuration written by system-config-firewall
# Manual customization of this file is not recommended.
*filter
:INPUT ACCEPT [0:0]
:FORWARD ACCEPT [0:0]
:OUTPUT ACCEPT [0:0]
-A INPUT -m state --state ESTABLISHED,RELATED -j ACCEPT
-A INPUT -p icmp -j ACCEPT
-A INPUT -i lo -j ACCEPT
-A INPUT -m state --state NEW -m tcp -p tcp --dport 22 -j ACCEPT
-A INPUT -j REJECT --reject-with icmp-host-prohibited
-A FORWARD -j REJECT --reject-with icmp-host-prohibited
COMMIT
```

Clicking the 'Disable' button and then 'Apply' in the Firewall Configuration Tool will disable the firewall. Most of the window will be grayed out. The 'Enable' button will become active, and the message in the lower right will read: "The firewall is disabled." When the firewall is disabled, it allows all traffic to pass in and out of the network. There is no trusted service or any blocked ports. In addition, there will be no '/etc/sysconfig/iptables' file.

```
[root@matthew ~]# cat /etc/sysconfig/iptables
cat: /etc/sysconfig/iptables: No such file or directory
```

After re-enabling the firewall, FTP (Port 21) is set as a trusted service. This causes a new rule to appear in the '/etc/sysconfig/iptables' file for Port 21. The new line is an INPUT rule for the FTP Service and makes this a trusted service. The system will now allow connections to port 21 used by the FTP service.

```
[root@matthew ~]# cat /etc/sysconfig/iptables
# Firewall configuration written by system-config-firewall
# Manual customization of this file is not recommended.
*filter
:INPUT ACCEPT [0:0]
:FORWARD ACCEPT [0:0]
:OUTPUT ACCEPT [0:0]
-A INPUT -m state --state ESTABLISHED,RELATED -j ACCEPT
-A INPUT -p icmp -j ACCEPT
-A INPUT -i lo -j ACCEPT
-A INPUT -m state --state NEW -m tcp -p tcp --dport 21 -j ACCEPT
-A INPUT -m state --state NEW -m tcp -p tcp --dport 22 -j ACCEPT
-A INPUT -j REJECT --reject-with icmp-host-prohibited
-A FORWARD -j REJECT --reject-with icmp-host-prohibited
COMMIT
```

The Firewall Configuration tool can configure some other simple rules, such as marking network interfaces which are trusted, masquerading IPv4 addresses, port forwarding, etc. You should take some time to investigate the tool yourself, but these options are likely beyond the scope of the exam.

Configure iptables rules

If you need some rules that are more complex than those that can be created using the Firewall Configuration tool, you should use the 'iptables' utility (or 'ip6tables' for configuring rules on an IPv6 network). The 'iptables' utility is a command line tool that is available in the Linux kernel 2.4 and above. It uses the Netfilter subsystem to enhance network connection, inspection, and processing. Features of the 'iptables' tool include: advanced logging, pre- and post-routing actions, network address translation, and port forwarding. The 'service iptables' command will list all available options for the iptables service.

```
[root@matthew ~]# service iptables
Usage: iptables {start|stop|restart|condrestart|status|panic|save}
```

The 'service' command can be used to determine if the iptables service is running or not. In the screenshot below, it displays the rules in effect, which means that the firewall is active.

```
[root@matthew ~]# service iptables status
Table: filter
Chain INPUT (policy ACCEPT)
num  target     prot opt source               destination
1    ACCEPT     all  --  0.0.0.0/0            0.0.0.0/0           state RELATED,
ESTABLISHED
2    ACCEPT     icmp --  0.0.0.0/0            0.0.0.0/0
3    ACCEPT     all  --  0.0.0.0/0            0.0.0.0/0
4    ACCEPT     tcp  --  0.0.0.0/0            0.0.0.0/0           state NEW tcp
dpt:21
5    ACCEPT     tcp  --  0.0.0.0/0            0.0.0.0/0           state NEW tcp
dpt:22
6    REJECT     all  --  0.0.0.0/0            0.0.0.0/0           reject-with ic
mp-host-prohibited

Chain FORWARD (policy ACCEPT)
num  target     prot opt source               destination
1    REJECT     all  --  0.0.0.0/0            0.0.0.0/0           reject-with ic
mp-host-prohibited

Chain OUTPUT (policy ACCEPT)
num  target     prot opt source               destination
```

You can stop or start the iptables service, using the command as shown below:

```
[root@matthew ~]# service iptables stop
iptables: Flushing firewall rules:                         [  OK  ]
iptables: Setting chains to policy ACCEPT: filter          [  OK  ]
iptables: Unloading modules:                               [  OK  ]

[root@matthew ~]# service iptables start
iptables: Applying firewall rules:                         [  OK  ]
iptables: Loading additional modules: nf_conntrack_ftp     [  OK  ]
```

Executing the following 'iptables' command as 'root' will list the rules of your firewall. The -L option is to list rules and the -n option is to display IP address and port in numeric format. The --line-numbers option causes iptables to provide a number at the far left. Line numbers are useful when adding or deleting rules.

```
[root@matthew ~]# iptables -L -n --line-numbers
Chain INPUT (policy ACCEPT)
num  target     prot opt source               destination
1    ACCEPT     all  --  0.0.0.0/0            0.0.0.0/0           state RELATED,
ESTABLISHED
2    ACCEPT     icmp --  0.0.0.0/0            0.0.0.0/0
3    ACCEPT     all  --  0.0.0.0/0            0.0.0.0/0
4    ACCEPT     tcp  --  0.0.0.0/0            0.0.0.0/0           state NEW tcp
dpt:21
5    ACCEPT     tcp  --  0.0.0.0/0            0.0.0.0/0           state NEW tcp
dpt:22
6    REJECT     all  --  0.0.0.0/0            0.0.0.0/0           reject-with ic
mp-host-prohibited

Chain FORWARD (policy ACCEPT)
num  target     prot opt source               destination
1    REJECT     all  --  0.0.0.0/0            0.0.0.0/0           reject-with ic
mp-host-prohibited

Chain OUTPUT (policy ACCEPT)
num  target     prot opt source               destination
```

The rule making FTP a trusted service is 4 as shown in the screenshot above. The iptables utility can delete that line with the -D option. After deleting the rule, running iptables again and searching for port 21 returns no results. However, the rule still exists in /etc/sysconfig/iptables.

```
[root@matthew ~]# iptables -D INPUT 4
[root@matthew ~]#
[root@matthew ~]# iptables -L -n --line-numbers | grep 21
[root@matthew ~]#
[root@matthew ~]# cat /etc/sysconfig/iptables | grep 21
-A INPUT -m state --state NEW -m tcp -p tcp --dport 21 -j ACCEPT
```

The rule still exists in the file because after deleting the rule it is necessary to save the rules configuration file (/etc/sysconfig/iptables). The 'service iptables save' command is used to save the new rules. After that, the rule no longer exists in the /etc/sysconfig/iptables file. However, even after the file has been saved the iptables service must be restarted so that it can re-read the new rules from the '/etc/sysconfig/iptables' file and enforce them.

```
[root@matthew ~]# service iptables save
iptables: Saving firewall rules to /etc/sysconfig/iptables:[  OK  ]
[root@matthew ~]# cat /etc/sysconfig/iptables | grep dpt:21
[root@matthew ~]#
[root@matthew ~]# service iptables restart
iptables: Flushing firewall rules:                         [  OK  ]
iptables: Setting chains to policy ACCEPT: filter          [  OK  ]
iptables: Unloading modules:                               [  OK  ]
iptables: Applying firewall rules:                         [  OK  ]
iptables: Loading additional modules: nf_conntrack_ftp     [  OK  ]
```

After deleting the FTP line, the current rules are:

```
[root@matthew ~]# iptables -L -n --line-numbers
Chain INPUT (policy ACCEPT)
num  target     prot opt source               destination
1    ACCEPT     all  --  0.0.0.0/0            0.0.0.0/0           state RELATED,
ESTABLISHED
2    ACCEPT     icmp --  0.0.0.0/0            0.0.0.0/0
3    ACCEPT     all  --  0.0.0.0/0            0.0.0.0/0
4    ACCEPT     tcp  --  0.0.0.0/0            0.0.0.0/0           state NEW tcp
dpt:22
5    REJECT     all  --  0.0.0.0/0            0.0.0.0/0           reject-with ic
mp-host-prohibited

Chain FORWARD (policy ACCEPT)
num  target     prot opt source               destination
1    REJECT     all  --  0.0.0.0/0            0.0.0.0/0           reject-with ic
mp-host-prohibited

Chain OUTPUT (policy ACCEPT)
num  target     prot opt source               destination
```

To add the FTP rule back with iptables into the same location (i.e. before line 4), the command would be:

```
[root@matthew ~]# iptables -I INPUT 4 -p tcp -m state --state NEW -m
tcp --dport 21 -j ACCEPT
```

```
[root@matthew ~]# iptables -L -n --line-numbers
Chain INPUT (policy ACCEPT)
num  target     prot opt source               destination
1    ACCEPT     all  --  0.0.0.0/0            0.0.0.0/0           state RELATED,
ESTABLISHED
2    ACCEPT     icmp --  0.0.0.0/0            0.0.0.0/0
3    ACCEPT     all  --  0.0.0.0/0            0.0.0.0/0
4    ACCEPT     tcp  --  0.0.0.0/0            0.0.0.0/0           state NEW tcp
dpt:21
5    ACCEPT     tcp  --  0.0.0.0/0            0.0.0.0/0           state NEW tcp
dpt:22
6    REJECT     all  --  0.0.0.0/0            0.0.0.0/0           reject-with ic
mp-host-prohibited

Chain FORWARD (policy ACCEPT)
num  target     prot opt source               destination
1    REJECT     all  --  0.0.0.0/0            0.0.0.0/0           reject-with ic
mp-host-prohibited

Chain OUTPUT (policy ACCEPT)
num  target     prot opt source               destination
```

Configuring complex firewall rules is an advanced topic. For the exam you need to understand the basic purposes of the iptables utility, the Firewall Configuration Tool, and their relationship to the /etc/sysconfig/iptables file.

Verify Common Vulnerabilities and Exposures (CVE) security updates are up to date

Common Vulnerabilities and Exposures (CVEs) is a dictionary of publicly known information security vulnerabilities and exposures. CVE's common identifiers enable data exchange between security products and provide a baseline index point for evaluating coverage of tools and services. Oracle strongly recommends that you frequently apply security updates and patches, to keep your Oracle Linux system secure.

There are several package management commands that can help you identify and install security updates on your Oracle Linux 6 system. The yum security plugin extends yum to allow lists and updates to be limited using security relevant criteria. This plugin must be installed and enabled in order to use the security-related package commands. The file '/etc/yum/pluginconf.d/security.conf' contains the configuration information for this plugin. It must contain the enabled=1 entry as shown below.

```
[root@matthew ~]# cat /etc/yum/pluginconf.d/security.conf
[main]
enabled=1
```

The available security-related package management commands provided by the plugin include:

- **yum --security check-update** -- Checks for security updates
- **yum --security update** -- Install only the security update packages on your Oracle Linux system.
- **yum list-security** -- List all available security updates with their CVE numbers.

- **yum updateinfo list security installed** -- List installed security updates.
- **yum updateinfo list security available** -- List available security updates.
- **yum updateinfo cves available** -- List all available CVEs.
- **yum updateinfo cves installed** -- List all installed CVEs.

Oracle Linux Support customers who have valid support contracts and CSI numbers for their Linux systems can also check the Errata and CVE information on the ULN website. The URLs for the errata and CVE listings are:

- **Errata listings** -- https://linux.oracle.com/errata
- **CVE Listings** -- https://linux.oracle.com/cve

The Errata page displays all the errata releases that are available. They are listed by type, severity, advisory, summary and release date. The results can be filtered by release and/or type (Bug, Security, and Enhancement). Selecting an item from the list provides additional details regarding the errata, including a description, related CVEs and the packages updated by the errata.

The CVE link provides information about security errata involving CVE identifiers. This site provides a summary of all CVEs offered through ULN. It is listed by CVE identifier and includes a brief synopsis and the release date. The list can be filtered by year. When a specific CVE identifier is selected, you will receive additional details, such as information on CVSS v2 metrics as well as affected platforms.

Oracle Linux System Monitoring and Troubleshooting

Use OSWatcher tool and configure to start at boot time

OS Watcher Black Box (OSWbb) is a collection of UNIX shell scripts intended to collect and archive operating system and network metrics to aid support in diagnosing performance issues. OSWbb operates as a set of background processes on the server and gathers data on a regular basis, invoking such Unix utilities as vmstat, netstat, iostat, and top. The OSWatcher.sh script spawns individual shell processes to collect specific kinds of data, using Unix operating system diagnostic utilities. The OSWbba analyzer can provide information on system slowdowns, system hangs and other performance problems. It also has the ability to graph data collected from iostat, netstat, and vmstat. In order to use OSWbba, Java version 1.4.2 or higher must be installed on your system. OSWbb is particularly useful for Oracle RAC (Real Application Clusters) and Oracle Grid Infrastructure configurations. The RAC-DDT (Diagnostic Data Tool) script file includes OSWbb, but does not install it by default. OSWbb invokes the following operating system utilities, each as a distinct background process, as data collectors. These utilities will be supported, or their equivalents, as available for each supported target platform.

- ps
- top
- mpstat
- iostat
- netstat
- traceroute
- vmstat

The OSWbb tool is available in two distributions:

- A Bourne shell version of OSWbb. The Bourne shell version will be able to run on any Oracle platform and OVM.

- An earlier version of OSWbb was written in ksh. Ksh is not installed by default on many UNIX/Linux platforms.

You can run the OSWatcher tool without specifying any options by running the startOSWbb.sh script. This will start the script with the default recording values. By default OSWbb records data at 30-second intervals, and maintains a rolling window of 48 hours (i.e. it will delete files more than 48 hours old). The frequency (in seconds) and duration (in hours) can be passed as arguments to the script.

```
# ./startOSWbb.sh [frequency duration]
```

The stopOSWbb.sh script will terminate all processes associated with OSWbb. This is the normal, graceful mechanism for stopping the tool's operation.

By default, the OSWatcher tool script collects all the data in the 'oswbb/archive' directory where it is installed. The location can be changed by setting the UNIX environment variable OSWWBB_ARCHIVE_DEST to the location desired before starting the tool. OSWbb will need access to the OS utilities: top, vmstat, iostat, mpstat, netstat, and traceroute. These OS utilities need to be installed on the system prior to running OSWbb. The user of OSWbb must also have execute permission on them.

OSWbb collects data in the following directories under the oswbb/archive directory:

- **oswiostat** -- Contains output from the iostat utility.
- **oswmeminfo** -- Contains a listing of the contents of /proc/meminfo.
- **oswmpstat** -- Contains output from the mpstat utility.
- **oswnetstat** -- Contains output from the netstat utility.
- **oswprvtnet** -- If you have enable private network tracing for RAC, contains information about the status of the private networks.
- **oswps** -- Contains output from the ps utility.

- **oswslabinfo** -- Contains a listing of the contents of /proc/slabinfo.
- **oswtop** -- Contains output from the top utility.
- **oswvmstat** -- Contains output from the vmstat utility.

Oracle Support recommends that you run and collect OSWatcher information for an extended period. Normally, in the event that the database node crashes, the system administrator needs to manually restart the OSWbb. However, there is a RPM supplied by Oracle that will automatically start OSWatcher for you at system startup. The file is available in the document: *'How To Start OSWatcher Black Box (OSWBB) Every System Boot [ID 580513.1]'*. After you download the oswbb-service RPM, install it with the rpm -ihv command.

Use sosreport

The sosreport utility collects configuration and diagnostic information from an Oracle Linux system. Some of the information collected includes the running kernel version, loaded modules, and system and service configuration files. In addition, it will run external programs to collect further information. The 'sosreport' utility is often used to assist in remote troubleshooting. The data collected is recorded in a compressed file that can be sent to a support representative. To run sosreport the sos package must be installed. The sos package is part of the default group and should be installed automatically. To verify that a system has the 'sosreport tool installed, you can run the following command as root:

```
[root@matthew ~]# which sosreport
/usr/sbin/sosreport
```

By default, the configuration information for the sosreport utility is stored in '/etc/sos.conf'. An example of the sos.conf file is below:

```
[root@matthew ~]# cat /etc/sos.conf
[general]

ftp_upload_url = ftp://ftp.oracle.com/support/incoming
smtp_server = None

[plugins]

#disable = rpm, selinux, dovecot

[tunables]

#rpm.rpmva = off
#general.syslogsize = 15
```

In the example below, the 'sosreport' tool is executed with the default options.

```
[root@matthew ~]# sosreport
```

The 'sosreport' tool gathers all of the information and stores it to a file, in this case:

```
Your sosreport has been generated and saved in:
  /tmp/sosreport-mmorris-20130927230423-3683.tar.xz
```

As the extension suggests, the report is saved as a tar.xz file. In order to view the individual files created by sosreport, the archive must be uncompressed by the 'xz' tool and then de-archived with the 'tar' command:

```
[root@matthew /]# cd /tmp
[root@matthew tmp]# xz -d sosreport-mmorris-20130927230423-
3683.tar.xz
[root@matthew tmp]# tar -xvf sosreport-mmorris-20130927230423-
3683.tar
```

Once the files have been dearchived, you can view the individual files containing the data that was collected by sosreport. Under the tmp directory (or whatever directory you uncompress the file in) will be a subdirectory matching the name and timestamp of the sosreport archive file. In this case, the subdirectory is 'mmorris-20130927230423'. The contents of that directory will look something like the following:

```
[root@matthew tmp]# cd matthew-20130927230313803374 03
[root@matthew matthew-2013092723031380337403]# ls
boot        hostname        lsof      root    sestatus      var
chkconfig   ifconfig        lspci     route   sos_commands  vgdisplay
date        installed-rpms  mount     sar19   sos_logs
df          java            netstat   sar20   sos_reports
dmidecode   lib             proc      sar24   sys
etc         lsb-release     ps        sar27   uname
free        lsmod           pstree    sbin    uptime
```

The screenshot below shows the contents of the uname, uptime, and sestatus files. The uname file contains information about the kernel. The uptime file provides system uptime information. The sestatus file provides information about the SELinux configuration.

```
[root@matthew matthew-2013092723031380337403]# cat uname
Linux matthew.example.com 2.6.39-200.24.1.el6uek.x86_64 #1 SMP Sat Jun 23 02:39:
07 EDT 2012 x86_64 x86_64 x86_64 GNU/Linux

[root@matthew matthew-2013092723031380337403]# cat uptime
 23:03:59 up  3:35,  2 users,  load average: 0.56, 0.14, 0.08

[root@matthew matthew-2013092723031380337403]# cat sestatus
SELinux status:                 enabled
SELinuxfs mount:                /selinux
Current mode:                   enforcing
Mode from config file:          enforcing
Policy version:                 26
Policy from config file:        targeted
```

To disable or skip a 'sosreport' plugin, run the command using the –n option. The below example skips the selinux plugin:

```
[root@matthew /]# sosreport -n selinux
```

Use sar, strace, iostat, tcpdump and ethereal tools

sar

The sar command produces system utilization reports based on the data collected by the System Activity Data Collector (sadc). As configured in Oracle Linux 6, sar is automatically run to process the files generated by sadc. The sadc command collects system utilization data and writes it to a file for later analysis. It is normally run by the sa1 script which is periodically invoked by cron via the file /etc/cron.d/sysstat. The sa1 script invokes sadc for a single one-second measuring interval and cron runs sa1 every 10 minutes by default. The data collected during each interval is added to the current /var/log/sa/sa<dd> file where <dd> is the two-digit representations of the current day's two-digit date.

In turn, sar is normally run by the sa2 script. This script is also periodically invoked by cron via the systat file. By default, cron runs sa2 once a day at 23:53, allowing it to produce a report for the entire day's files from sadc. The sar report files are written to /var/log/sa/ and are named sar<dd>, where <dd> is the two-digit representations of the two-digit date of the day represented by the sadc files.

The format of a sar report produced by the default Oracle Linux configuration consists of multiple sections. Each section contains a specific type of data and is ordered by the time of day that the data was collected. Since sadc is configured to perform a one-second measurement interval every ten minutes, the default sar reports contain data in ten-minute increments, from 00:00 to 23:50. The sections start with a heading describing the data they contain and the heading is repeated at regular intervals. Each section ends with a line containing the average of the data reported in them.

Executing the sar command with no parameters produces a CPU utilization report. This is often one of the first facilities run to diagnose a problem because it monitors major system resources. If CPU utilization is near 100 percent, the workload sampled is CPU-bound. The following example runs the sar CPU utilization report three times at an interval of three seconds:

```
[root@matthew sa]# sar 3 3
Linux 2.6.39-200.24.1.el6uek.x86_64 (matthew.example.com)        09/28/2013
x86_64_  (1 CPU)

10:46:22 AM     CPU     %user     %nice   %system   %iowait    %steal     %idle
10:46:25 AM     all      0.33      0.00      0.67      0.00      0.00     99.00
10:46:28 AM     all      0.34      0.00      0.34      0.34      0.00     98.99
10:46:31 AM     all      0.66      0.00      0.66      0.00      0.00     98.67
Average:        all      0.44      0.00      0.56      0.11      0.00     98.89
```

The -o option of sar can be used to capture the output into a file. In the example below, the output is captured in binary form in the /tmp/sar.out file.

```
[root@matthew sa]# sar -o /tmp/sar.out 3 3
Linux 2.6.39-200.24.1.el6uek.x86_64 (matthew.example.com)       09/28/2013
x86_64_  (1 CPU)

10:49:59 AM     CPU     %user     %nice   %system   %iowait    %steal     %idle
10:50:02 AM     all      0.67      0.00      1.67      0.33      0.00     97.32
10:50:05 AM     all      0.33      0.00      1.33      0.67      0.00     97.67
10:50:08 AM     all      0.33      0.00      1.66      0.66      0.00     97.34
Average:        all      0.44      0.00      1.56      0.56      0.00     97.44
```

Because the output is in binary form, it cannot be read with a text editor. To read the output that was stored in the /tmp/sar.out file, the sar command is executed with the –f option as shown below.

```
[root@matthew sa]# sar -f /tmp/sar.out
Linux 2.6.39-200.24.1.el6uek.x86_64 (matthew.example.com)       09/28/2013
x86_64_  (1 CPU)

10:49:59 AM     CPU     %user     %nice   %system   %iowait    %steal     %idle
10:50:02 AM     all      0.67      0.00      1.67      0.33      0.00     97.32
10:50:05 AM     all      0.33      0.00      1.33      0.67      0.00     97.67
10:50:08 AM     all      0.33      0.00      1.66      0.66      0.00     97.34
Average:        all      0.44      0.00      1.56      0.56      0.00     97.44
```

While the default sar option is the CPU utilization report, there are a number of other statistics that can be gathered, including:

- **-b** -- Report I/O and transfer rate statistics.
- **-B** -- Report paging statistics.
- **-d** -- Report activity for each block device
- **-m** -- Report power management statistics.
- **-q** -- Report queue length and load averages.
- **-r** -- Report memory utilization statistics.
- **-R** -- Report memory statistics.
- **-S** -- Report swap space utilization statistics.
- **-u** -- Report CPU utilization.
- **-v** -- Report status of inode, file and other kernel tables.

strace

The strace rool is a command-line utility for diagnosis and debugging that can be used to trace system calls that are made and received by a running process. It records the name of each system call, its arguments, return value, signals received by the process and other interactions with the kernel. The utility then prints this information to standard error output or to a selected file.

In the example below 'gedit' is executed in the background. Then the 'ps' command is used to get the process ID. With the process id, it is possible to execute 'strace' against the running process to capture the output and store it to a file. Once a few second of data have been collected, strace is terminated with Control-C.

```
[root@matthew sa]# gedit &
[1] 4690
[root@matthew sa]# ps -ef | grep gedit
root      4690  2578  2 15:29 pts/0    00:00:00 gedit
root      4695  2578  0 15:30 pts/0    00:00:00 grep gedit
[root@matthew sa]# strace -o /tmp/strace_gedit.out -p 4690
Process 4690 attached - interrupt to quit
^CProcess 4690 detached
```

It is also possible to run strace while lanching a process. This is often used to diagnose why a process is failing to start. To run 'strace' when you launch a process/application, the command is very similar to the above, but the name of the application to be executed is used instead of the '-p' option and process id. In the example below, the 'gedit' editor is started with system call tracing using the ‘strace’ command.

```
[root@matthew sa]# strace -o /tmp/strace_gedit2.out gedit
```

A snippet of the /tmp/strace_gedit2.out file is shown below. Interpreting strace files is outside the scope of the exam (or this guide).

```
execve("/usr/bin/gedit", ["gedit"], [/* 46 vars */]) = 0
brk(0)                                  = 0x246b000
mmap(NULL, 4096, PROT_READ|PROT_WRITE, MAP_PRIVATE|MAP_ANONYMOUS, -1, 0) = 0x7f6
58fe71000
access("/etc/ld.so.preload", R_OK)      = -1 ENOENT (No such file or directory)
open("/etc/ld.so.cache", O_RDONLY)      = 3
fstat(3, {st_mode=S_IFREG|0644, st_size=55682, ...}) = 0
mmap(NULL, 55682, PROT_READ, MAP_PRIVATE, 3, 0) = 0x7f658fe63000
close(3)                                = 0
open("/usr/lib64/libxml2.so.2", O_RDONLY) = 3
read(3, "\177ELF\2\1\1\0\0\0\0\0\0\0\0\0\3\0>\0\1\0\0\0\360\306\2\2065\0\0\0"...
, 832) = 832
```

iostat

The iostat command displays an overview of CPU utilization, along with I/O statistics for one or more disk drives. It monitors system input/output device loading by observing the time the devices are active in relation to their average transfer rates. Executing 'iostat' with no options will show CPU and device statistics since the time the system was booted.

```
[root@matthew sa]# iostat
Linux 2.6.39-200.24.1.el6uek.x86_64 (matthew.example.com)       09/28/2013
x86_64_ (1 CPU)

avg-cpu:  %user   %nice %system %iowait  %steal   %idle
           0.71    0.00    0.84    1.37    0.00   97.08

Device:            tps   Blk_read/s   Blk_wrtn/s   Blk_read   Blk_wrtn
sda               4.02       223.43       142.69    5299918    3384844
sdb               0.03         0.21         0.00       5058          8
sdc               0.03         0.21         0.00       4952          0
sdd               0.04         0.28         0.00       6712          0
dm-0              4.92       222.53       141.72    5278690    3361800
dm-1              0.18         0.50         0.97      11848      23000
```

The CPU utilization report includes the following percentages:

- **User** -- Percentage of time spent in user mode (running applications, etc.)
- **Nice** -- Percentage of time spent in user mode (for processes that have altered their scheduling priority using nice)
- **System** -- Percentage of time spent in kernel mode

- **Iowait** -- Percentage of time that the CPU or CPUs were idle during which the system had an outstanding disk I/O request.
- **Steal** -- Percentage of time spent in involuntary wait by the virtual CPU or CPUs while the hypervisor was servicing another virtual processor.
- **Idle** -- Percentage of time spent idle

The device utilization report has one line for each active disk device on the system and includes the following information:

- **Device** -- The device specification.
- **Tps** -- The number of transfers (or I/O operations) per second.
- **Blk_Reads/s** -- The number of 512-byte blocks read per second.
- **Blk_wrtn/s** -- The number of 512-byte blocks written per second.
- **Blk_read** -- The total number of 512-byte blocks read.
- **Blk_wrtn** -- The total number of 512-byte block written.

The iostat options can be used to display portions of the report:

- **–c** -- Display just the CPU utilization report
- **–d** -- Display just the devices report.
- **–p** -- Provide a specific device name to display in the report.

tcpdump

The tcpdump utility is a powerful command line interface packet sniffer. It acts as a network analysis tool that prints out a description of the contents of packets on a network interface. The tool is useful for investigating TCP/IP packets and diagnosing network related issues. The utility allows you to capture network traffic based on specified filters.

Executing tcpdump with the -D option will display the list of network interfaces:

```
[root@matthew sa]# tcpdump -D
1.eth0
2.eth1
3.usbmon1 (USB bus number 1)
4.any (Pseudo-device that captures on all interfaces)
5.lo
```

The following example captures all traffic for the HTTP protocol via TCP port 80. After starting tcpdump, the Firefox browser is opened and numerous packets are captured by tcpdump. The screenshot below is just a fraction of the ones received:

```
[root@matthew sa]# tcpdump port 80
tcpdump: verbose output suppressed, use -v or -vv for full protocol decode
listening on eth0, link-type EN10MB (Ethernet), capture size 65535 bytes
16:03:51.302962 IP 10.0.2.15.20718 > yh-in-f147.1e100.net.http: Flags [S], seq 1
716182862, win 14600, options [mss 1460,sackOK,TS val 27299488 ecr 0,nop,wscale
7], length 0
16:03:51.920753 IP 10.0.2.15.20719 > yh-in-f147.1e100.net.http: Flags [S], seq 1
957832739, win 14600, options [mss 1460,sackOK,TS val 27300105 ecr 0,nop,wscale
7], length 0
16:03:51.963821 IP yh-in-f147.1e100.net.http > 10.0.2.15.20718: Flags [S.], seq
563840001, ack 1716182863, win 65535, options [mss 1460], length 0
16:03:51.963909 IP 10.0.2.15.20718 > yh-in-f147.1e100.net.http: Flags [.], ack 1
, win 14600, length 0
16:03:51.964407 IP 10.0.2.15.20718 > yh-in-f147.1e100.net.http: Flags [P.], seq
1:587, ack 1, win 14600, length 586
16:03:51.964929 IP yh-in-f147.1e100.net.http > 10.0.2.15.20718: Flags [.], ack 5
87, win 65535, length 0
```

To capture the network traffic output to a file, you can use the –w option and specify the file name. In the example below, the output is captured in the '/tmp/tcpdump_http.out' file.

```
[root@matthew sa]# tcpdump port 80 -w /tmp/tcpdump_http.out
tcpdump: listening on eth0, link-type EN10MB (Ethernet), capture size
65535 bytes
^C46 packets captured
46 packets received by filter
0 packets dropped by kernel
```

The files created by tcpdump are binary and cannot be read with a text editor. To read a file in which network traffic data was captured, you can use the –r option of the tcpdump command:

```
[root@matthew sa]# tcpdump -r /tmp/tcpdump_http.out
reading from file /tmp/tcpdump_http.out, link-type EN10MB (Ethernet)
16:09:26.297529 IP 10.0.2.15.61966 > atl14s08-in-f17.1e100.net.http:
Flags [S], seq 2058858418, win 14600, options [mss 1460,sackOK,TS val
27634482 ecr 0,nop,wscale 7], length 0
...
```

The –v, -vv, and -vvv options will increase the verbosity level of the data captured. As with the output from strace, reading the files created by tcpdump is beyond the scope of the exam.

ethereal

Ethereal is now Wireshark. The purpose of Wireshark (ethereal) is essentially the same as tcpdump -- they are both network protocol analyzer tools. Wireshark goes beyond the capabilities of tcpdump in that it lets you interactively browse the network traffic that has been captured from a computer network. In order to use Wireshark, the Wireshark RPM package must be installed on Oracle Linux. Installing Wireshark itself ('yum install wireshark') will install the command line tool tethereal and other binaries. There is also a GUI package, 'wireshark-gnome'. Installing this provides a more user-friendly interface for viewing the network packets. It lets you interactively browse packet data from a live network or from a previously saved capture file. Wireshark's native capture file format is libpcap format, which is also the format used by tcpdump and various other tools.

The 'tethereal' tool is the command line tool that can be used to dump and analyze network traffic. Similat to tcpdump, you can display the network interfaces available on the system, with the –D option of the 'tethereal' command:

```
[root@matthew sa]# tethereal -D
1. eth0
2. eth1
3. usbmon1 (USB bus number 1)
4. any (Pseudo-device that captures on all interfaces)
5. lo
```

The Wireshark GUI can be started from the command line by executing the command '/usr/sbin/wireshark'. Alternatively, you can also find this application under the Applications -> Internet ->Wireshark Network Analyzer menu. Once the main screen comes up, you can select an interface such as eth0 and start the capture of network packets. The following screenshot shows a running capture from eth0:

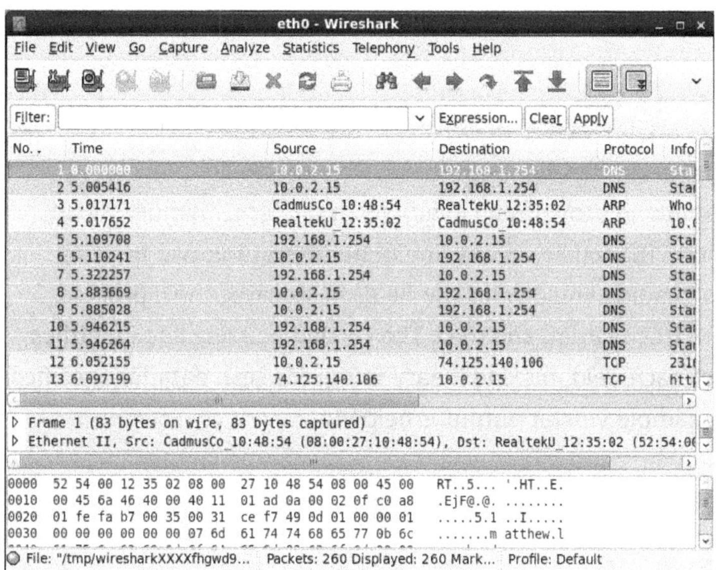

You can click the Filter button and select a specific type of packet to filter for, such as HTTP, IP, or UDP only.

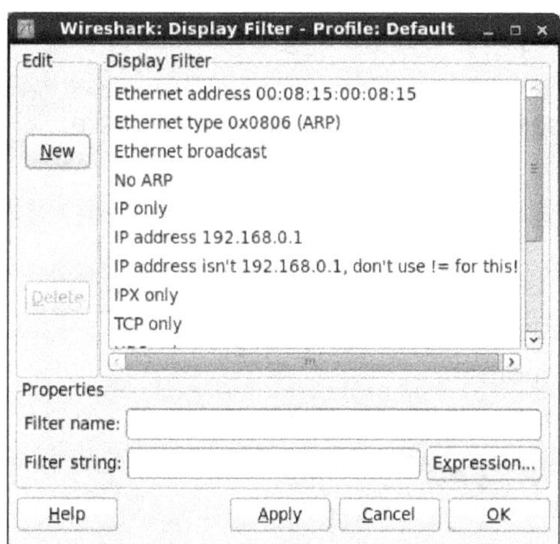

The data collected by Wireshark clearly shows the Source IP, Destination IP, and Protocol IP information for all packets. You can sort based on Destination IP or any other fields. The output can be saved in a file and opened at a later for analysis. The Wireshark tool can read network data captured in several formats like libcap, tcpdump, and snoop. Wireshark will automatically determine the file format when opening the file.

Use vmstat and top

vmstat

The vmstat command provides an overview of process, memory, swap, I/O, system, and CPU activity in one line of numbers (and two heading lines). The top heading line divides the fields in six categories: process, memory, swap, I/O, system, and CPU. The second heading line identifies the contents of each field, making it easy to quickly scan data for specific statistics. An example vmstat output is below:

```
[root@matthew sa]# vmstat
procs -----------memory---------- ---swap-- -----io---- --system-- -----cpu-----
 r  b   swpd   free   buff  cache   si   so    bi    bo   in   cs us sy id wa st
 0  0  10796 208332  25940 485948    0    0    95    54   83  135  1  1 97  1  0
```

The process-related fields are:

- **r** -- The number of runnable processes waiting for access to the CPU
- **b** -- The number of processes in an uninterruptible sleep state

The memory-related fields are:

- **swpd** -- The amount of virtual memory used
- **free** -- The amount of free memory
- **buff** -- The amount of memory used for buffers
- **cache** -- The amount of memory used as page cache

The swap-related fields are:

- **si** -- The amount of memory swapped in from disk
- **so** -- The amount of memory swapped out to disk

The I/O-related fields are:

- **bi** -- Blocks sent to a block device
- **bo** -- Blocks received from a block device

The system-related fields are:

- **in** -- The number of interrupts per second
- **cs** -- The number of context switches per second

The CPU-related fields are:

- **us** -- The percentage of the time the CPU ran user-level code
- **sy** -- The percentage of the time the CPU ran system-level code
- **id** -- The percentage of the time the CPU was idle
- **wa** -- I/O wait
- **st** -- The percentage of real cpu allocated to tasks other than running your Virtual Machine

When vmstat is executed with no options, only a single result line is returned. The line contains averages, calculated from the time the system was last booted. In general, system admins do not rely on the data in this line, as the time over which it was collected varies. More meaningful data can be generated by using vmstat's ability to repetitively display resource utilization data at set intervals. For example, the command vmstat 1 displays one new line of utilization data every second. The command 'vmstat 2 4' will display one new line every two seconds and four iterations (i.e. eight seconds of data). The following screenshot shows an example of this:

```
[root@matthew sa]# vmstat 2 4
procs -----------memory---------- ---swap-- -----io---- --system-- -----cpu-----
 r  b   swpd   free   buff  cache   si   so    bi    bo   in   cs us sy id wa st
 0  0  10796 209784  26060 486020    0    0    94    53   83  135  1  1 97  1  0
 1  0  10796 177296  26060 486248    0    0    88     0  408 1117 13 19 67  2  0
 2  0  10796 139484  26068 486792    0    0    72    54  613 1556 16 23 58  3  0
 0  0  10796 134128  26076 487028    0    0   130    40  506  614 23 15 58  4  0
```

top

The top command does a little bit of everything. CPU utilization, process statistics, memory utilization -- top monitors it all. It provides a dynamic real time view of a Linux system. Top is very useful for identifying system performance related issues. The following screenshot shows the top several lines of a top screen.

```
top - 17:33:54 up  9:10,  2 users,  load average: 0.16, 0.11, 0.07
Tasks: 143 total,   1 running, 142 sleeping,   0 stopped,   0 zombie
Cpu(s):  1.3%us,  8.6%sy,  0.0%ni, 89.1%id,  1.0%wa,  0.0%hi,  0.0%si,  0.0%st
Mem:   1020876k total,   918260k used,   102616k free,    26320k buffers
Swap:  2064380k total,    10912k used,  2053468k free,   498416k cached

  PID USER      PR  NI  VIRT  RES  SHR S %CPU %MEM    TIME+  COMMAND
 5202 root      20   0  694m 115m  26m S  7.6 11.6   0:29.98 firefox
 1991 root      20   0  132m  29m 6724 S  0.7  2.9   0:39.07 Xorg
 5257 root      20   0 15080 1136  844 R  0.7  0.1   0:00.07 top
   22 root      39  19     0    0    0 S  0.3  0.0   0:01.74 khugepaged
 1579 haldaemo  20   0 26352 1936 1296 S  0.3  0.2   0:01.56 hald
 2203 root      20   0  197m 1168  648 S  0.3  0.1   1:45.99 VBoxClient
 2263 root      20   0  516m  15m 8540 S  0.3  1.5   0:12.96 nautilus
```

Whereas the vmstat command requires parameters to provide more than one iteration, top requires a parameter to stop. Running the top command with the –n option will exit the utility after n iterations. Without this option, the top command continues displaying the real time system activity until stopped by pressing 'q' or Control-C.

```
[root@matthew /]# top -n 3
```

To display the processes or activity of a particular user on the system, run the top command with –u option. In the example below, the activity of use 'jjones' will be reported by top:

```
[root@matthew /]# top -u jjones
```

By default top sorts processes based on CPU usage. The utility is interactive and will respond to various key commands. Typing an upper case M while viewing top will cause the process to be re-sorted based on memory (%MEM). There are several other interactive options for sorting, including the following:

- **A** -- start time
- **M** -- %MEM
- **N** -- PID
- **P** -- %CPU
- **T** -- TIME+

Describe DTrace tool

DTrace is a comprehensive dynamic tracing facility. It was first developed for the Oracle Solaris operating system, but has been ported to Oracle Linux. The output from DTrace can be used to track down performance problems across many layers of software, or to locate the causes of aberrant behavior. DTrace allows you to record data at locations of interest in the kernel, called probes. A probe is a location to which DTrace can bind a request to perform a set of actions, such as recording a stack trace, a timestamp, or the argument to a function. Probes function like programmable sensors that record information.

When the probe is triggered, DTrace gathers data from it and reports it back. Dtrace has a programming language called D that can be used to query the system probes. With it, you can get immediate, concise answers to arbitrary questions that you formulate. DTrace and the D programming language are an enormous topic that cannot be covered in a brief chapter. Based on the exam topic, you need to have a basic understanding of DTrace's role.

Set up kdump / netconsole

kdump

Kdump is an advanced crash dumping mechanism. When kdump is enabled, the system is booted from the context of another kernel. The second kernel reserves a small amount of memory that is designed to capture the core dump image in the event of a system crash. If there is a system crash and no core dump exists to analyze, it is very difficult to determine the exact cause of the system failure. For this reason, it is strongly recommended that you have this feature enabled.

There are two ways that the kdump service is commonly configured:

- When FirstBoot tool is run after initial installation
- Using the Kernel Dump Configuration graphical utility

The GUI utility can be launched from the System -> Administration -> Kernel crash dumps option if the system has the Desktop GUI packages installed. The utility can also be lauched by executing system-config-kdump at the command line. In the example screenshot below, the utility shows that kdump is not currently enabled.

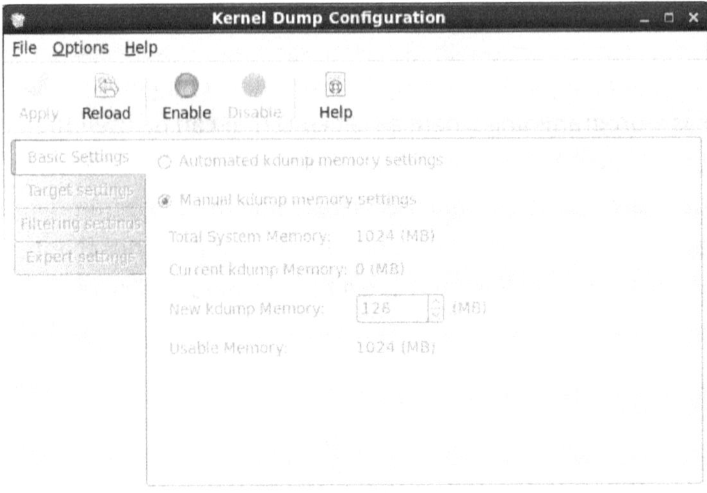

Once kdump has been enabled, the GUI has tabs that allow you to configure Basic settings, Target settings, Filtering settings, and Expert settings. The tabs allow you configure aspects of kdump such as:

- Amount of memory reserved for kdump
- The default location where the vmcore file is created upon a crash
- The level of information included in the vmcore file

The system must be rebooted if kdump is enabled from a disabled state or if some of the parameters are altered (such as the amount of memory reserved for kdump). The configuration file for the kdump crash collection service is '/etc/kdump.conf'. This is where the kdump configuration information is stored. The file is too large to display here effectively. You should open it on your Linux test system with an ASCII file viewer. You can determine the status of the kdump service using the following command:

```
[root@matthew sa]# service kdump status
Kdump is not operational
```

netconsole

The 'netconsole' utility provides a means for system console messages to be redirected across a network to another server. When a Linux system experiences critical or fatal issues, console messages are often lost due to the system crash. If that happens, it is it not possible to retrieve the logs of the incident which caused the issue from the affected system, making it more difficult to debug.

It is possible to configure the Netconsole utility to send/redirect system console messages over the network to a designated server in the event of a fatal issue. It is a light-weight and non-intrusive logging capture tool. There are two systems involved in setting up netconsole:

- Netconsole Server –- system that receives the console messages
- Netconsole Client –- system that sends the console messages to configured server

Verify proper creation of vmcore by kdump using crash

The crash utility allows you to analyze the state of the Oracle Linux system while it is running. It can also analyze a core dump has been created by the netdump, diskdump, kdump, or xendump facilities due to a kernel crash. The crash utility is installed by default on Oracle Linux 6. You can verify that it is installed by using the 'which' command:

```
[root@matthew /]# which crash
/usr/bin/crash
```

In order to analyze crash dumps on Oracle Linux 6 systems, you must have the kerneldebuginfo packages that match the version of the kernel that you are running. The 'uname -r' command will provide the specific kernel version you are running:

```
[root@matthew /]# uname -r
2.6.39-200.24.1.el6uek.x86_64
```

The kernel-debuginfo packages corresponding to the 2.6.39-200.24.1.el6uek.x86_64 kernel are required to run crash against a vmcore file generated on this system. The kernel-debuginfo RPM packages are available at: https://oss.oracle.com/ol6/debuginfo/. Since uname indicates the system is running a UEK kernel, the following commands will download the required RPMs to the system. Because the 'uname -r' command is embedded into the commands, it will download the specific rpm required.

```
[root@matthew /]# export DLP="https://oss.oracle.com/ol6/debuginfo"
[root@matthew /]# wget ${DLP}/kernel-uek-debuginfo-`uname -r`.rpm
[root@matthew /]# wget ${DLP}/kernel-uek-debuginfo-common-`uname -
r`.rpm
```

Once the debuginfo and debuginfo-common packages have been doqnloaded, they must be installed on the system using the rpm utility:

```
[root@matthew /]# rpm -Uhv kernel-uek-debuginfo-2.6.39-
200.24.1.el6uek.x86_64.rpm \
kernel-uek-debuginfo-common-2.6.39-200.24.1.el6uek.x86_64.rpm
```

Once the crash utility and the kernel-debuginfo RPM packages are installed on a system, if it experiences a crash a vmcore file for the crash will be created. The file will be inside a time-stamped directory under the '/var/crash' directory. It is possible to force a crash that will verify that a vmcore file gets generated. Verifying that everything is working is important. If something is not correct, waiting until a real crash occurs to find out is not a viable option. The commands below that will force a crash should be executed at runlevel 3 (and obviously <u>not</u> on a production system that is currently in use). To take your system to runlevel 3, execute the following command:

```
[root@matthew /]# init 3
```

Login to your Oracle Linux 6 system as the 'root' user and run the following commands:

```
[root@matthew /]# echo 1 > /proc/sys/kernel/sysrq
[root@matthew /]# echo c > /proc/sysrq-trigger
```

The above commands will cause the system to crash and create a vmcore file in the directory specified by the ‘path’ variable in /etc/kdump.conf (/var/crash in this case). You can use the system-config-kdump utility to view or change the path for the vmcore file. The system will reboot automatically after the core file has been created:

```
[root@matthew ~]# cd /var/crash
[root@matthew crash]# ls
127.0.0.1-2013-09-28-20:16:42
[root@matthew crash]# cd 127.0.0.1-2013-09-28-20\:16\:42/
[root@matthew 127.0.0.1-2013-09-28-20:16:42]# ls -l
total 28852
-rw-------. 1 root root 29536922 Sep 28 20:16 vmcore
[root@matthew 127.0.0.1-2013-09-28-20:16:42]#
```

Executing the 'crash' command with the –osrelease option will display the OS release information of the vmcore file. The core file must be analyzed using the matching version kernel-debuginfo files. You can check them by running the rpm utility with the -qa options and filtering for uek-debug with the grep command.

```
[root@matthew 127.0.0.1-2013-09-28…]# crash --osrelease vmcore
2.6.39-200.24.1.el6uek.x86_64
[root@matthew 127.0.0.1-2013-09-28…]# rpm -qa | grep uek-debug
kernel-uek-debuginfo-2.6.39-200.24.1.el6uek.x86_64
kernel-uek-debuginfo-common-2.6.39-200.24.1.el6uek.x86_64
```

Debugging system crash files is an advanced topic beyond what is required for the exam.

Describe OS management capabilities of both Opscenter and EM management for Oracle Linux

Oracle Enterprise Manager Cloud Control and Oracle Enterprise Manager Ops Center work together to provide a complete data center management solution. Both products monitor managed assets but at different levels of the data center asset stack. Oracle Enterprise Manager Cloud Control manages applications, middleware, and databases. Oracle Enterprise Manager Ops Center manages operating systems, virtual machines, servers, storage resources, and network resources. Oracle Enterprise Manager Ops Center allows you to provision, update (patch), monitor, and manage the physical and virtual managed assets in multiple data centers from a single console, regardless of where the asset is located.

Ops Center is included free with:

- Oracle Linux Network / Basic / Premier Support
- Oracle Premier Support for Systems
- Oracle Premier Support for Operating Systems

The Oracle Enterprise Manager Ops Center software provides features tailored for administrating the data center infrastructure, including the following:

- **Dashboards** -- View a summary of a group of assets or an individual asset, including a graphical representation of the status and membership.
- **Incident management** -- Monitors the assets according to rules and thresholds that you set. If an incident occurs, the incident knowledge base is activated to display known issues and the assigned administrators in the Message Center.
- **Integration with Oracle Enterprise Manager Cloud Control** -- View configuration, health, and performance information and incidents of managed assets using either software product. Changes in one product are reported in the other product.
- **Profiles for assets** -- Creates software profiles and operational profiles that contain your custom executable scripts and include them in a plan.
- **Operational plans** -- Deploys a single script as an operational profile. An operational plan runs as an individual plan, or as a step within a deployment plan. Run the scripts independent of local software, and use them to perform specific tasks in your environment, such as configuration options, or to assist in incident management.
- **Deployment plans** -- Combines one or more profiles and scripts to create a multi-task plan that provisions operating systems or firmware efficiently and consistently.
- **Plan management** -- Provides default templates, profiles, and plans needed to create and deploy plans. Plan management also

includes an Incidents Knowledge Base, where you can create a database of known issues. Use operational profiles and annotations to associate recommended or automated actions to respond to known issues.

- **Hardware management** -- Updates system component firmware and tracks hardware configuration changes over time. Increase energy efficiency by tracking energy utilization for ILOM x64, ILOM CMT, and M-Series servers and chassis and manages the power budget of ILOM 3.0 systems.
- **Virtualization management** -- Manages virtual assets such as Oracle Solaris Zones, Oracle VM Servers for SPARC, Oracle VM Servers for x86, and their guests. The network and storage resources for virtual assets are provided by their membership in server pools.
- **Reports** -- Creates reports for assets and activities and export the reports as files in PDF format or as comma-delimited values.

ABOUT THE AUTHOR

Matthew Morris is an Oracle Database Administrator and Developer currently employed as a Database Engineer with Computer Sciences Corporation. Matthew has worked with the Oracle database since 1996 when he worked in the RDBMS support team for Oracle Support Services. Employed with Oracle for over eleven years in support and development positions, Matthew was an early adopter of the Oracle Certified Professional program. He was one of the first one hundred Oracle Certified Database Administrators (version 7.3) and in the first hundred to become an Oracle Certified Forms Developer. In the years since, he has upgraded his Database Administrator certification for releases 8i, 9i, 10G and 11G, become an Oracle Advanced PL/SQL Developer Certified Professional and added the Expert certifications for Application Express, SQL, and SQL Tuning. Outside of Oracle, he has CompTIA certifications in Linux+ and Security+.

www.ingramcontent.com/pod-product-compliance
Lightning Source LLC
Chambersburg PA
CBHW071155050326
40689CB00011B/2124